THE FIGHTER
Within

ROCKY WARREN

THE FIGHTER
Within

ROCKY WARREN

EBURY
PRESS

An Ebury Press book
Published by Random House Australia Pty Ltd
Level 3, 100 Pacific Highway, North Sydney NSW 2060
www.randomhouse.com.au

First published by Ebury Press in 2009

Addresses for companies within the Random House Group can be found
at www.randomhouse.com.au/offices

National Library of Australia
Cataloguing-in-Publication Entry

Warren, Rocky.
The fighter within.

ISBN 978 1 74166 665 6 (pbk).

Self-realisation.
Success.
Conduct of life.

158.1

Cover design by Dave Altheim
Internal design by Midland Typesetters
Typeset by Midland Typesetters, Australia
Printed and bound by Griffin Press, South Australia

Random House Australia uses papers that are natural, renewable and
recyclable products and made from wood grown in sustainable forests.
The logging and manufacturing processes are expected to conform to the
environmental regulations of the country of origin.

10 9 8 7 6 5 4 3 2 1

I dedicate this book to Darrel and Carol, my brother and my friend, both taken away from my life well before I would have liked. Together we'll still grow old.

CONTENTS

THE WARM-UP

This is the time a fighter clears his mind of all thoughts except the ensuing fight. I go over in my mind again and again how fit I am, and remind myself how important it is to win this fight. STRAIGHT LEFT. Of course I have butterflies in my stomach . . . all good fighters get those. But I know I have the skills and the belief in myself to win this fight. RIGHT CROSS. I've trained hard and now nothing except my opponent can stop me from achieving the success I so rightly deserve.

Just like Sylvester Stallone, Rocky is not my real name, but it's the one that everybody knows me by. Rocky Warren is the name I used throughout my professional boxing career, and one I haven't been able to drop.

My ring nickname was 'The Fighting Machine', and my greatest claim to fame was as a sparring partner to three-time world champion Jeff Fenech, prior to him winning his second world title. I had 48 professional bouts and held a state title at feather-weight before I retired from boxing at the ripe old age of 27. I was nine stone back then . . . I'm a little heavier than that now.

I'm not religious, although I did go to church when I was a kid. I'm from a poor, working-class family who didn't have much, but I don't remember missing out on too much while growing up.

I was married at 21, and after the honeymoon we

moved into our first home, which cost $47,900. A few years later, my wife and I had two children, Matt and Kristi. My life was good. Nothing really out of the ordinary. It had its ups and downs, just like the lives of most people. But that was then . . .

Today, I'm 47 years old. I've been divorced for 17 years. I live in a Sydney penthouse with the most spectacular views of the city and Harbour Bridge. I also own the penthouse next door.

I live alone. My partner gives me the space I need and allows me to be me. This may sound a little selfish; however, the arrangement seems to work for her just as well. She is my driving force, my guiding light, my inspiration to continue to grow.

I drive a brand new Mercedes-Benz. I have a holiday home on the water at Sanctuary Cove, one of Queensland's most prestigious suburbs, as well as other investment properties.

I own and run one of Sydney's largest home loan centres. The office fit-out has been compared to a Palazzo Versace hotel.

My love life is perfect. I work out at the gym every day and live a healthy, happy life. I spend quality time with my grown-up children who I adore; and my relationships with both family and friends are genuine and beautiful. I live a blessed life, but . . .

I know there's more. Until recently, I believed that everything I have I earned through hard work and persistence. I now realise I'm wrong.

There is a higher power, one that can multiply what I have and what I've done millions of times. Don't get me wrong, I haven't found religion, nor do I intend to anytime soon. But I have found something that is all-powerful and all-conquering. It has expanded my heart and removed the boundaries from my mind. It lets me see my future life in advance . . . and I like what I see.

I haven't found God or had a spiritual awakening. But like Arnold Schwarzenegger, I feel like I've had a 'total recall'.

It's as if I've been recalled for a total overhaul of everything I've ever thought was true and correct, and I now realise that there is no limit to how much money or love I can have in my life, or to how much good I can bring to the world.

If I accept my 'recall' with open arms and change my thinking to correspond with the pictures in my mind, anything and everything is both possible and probable.

What I've found are the 'Laws of the Universe'. Many hundreds of thousands of people have already been exposed to one of these Laws – the Law of Attraction – through Rhonda Byrne's *The Secret*. I've spoken with people who claim the knowledge of these Laws has changed their lives, and there are now thousands of wonderful stories surfacing all around the world that validate the Laws' theories.

Throughout the journey of this book, I will touch

on just a few of these Laws, including the Law of Nature, the Law of Giving, the Law of Thinking, the Law of Gravity, the Law of Compensation, the Law of Supply, the Law of Increase and the Law of Non-resistance. I'll explain to you my understanding of these Laws, and how people who truly understand and accept them have used them to great advantage in their lives.

From my studies, what I now understand is that there is an abundance of money, an abundance of love, an abundance of knowledge, and an abundance of everything in our world, if we're prepared to receive it.

While I can't explain the Universal Laws as a theologian, or a pastor, or a scientist, or even as an extremely intelligent human being, what I can do is teach you in simple, layman's terms my understanding of these Laws and how they affect you and your life. So, in the following ten rounds I will show you how to slay your 'real-life dragons' and how to put yourself in a place where only prosperity survives.

You can have as much money as you want. You can have better health, more love, greater self-confidence, less stress, increased weight-loss and a more prosperous life, if you can open your mind and be accepting of what you're about to read.

I want to help you to realise that you can have whatever you want, whenever you want it.

At the time of writing this book, my net worth is

around $5 million. Over the next two years I intend to give at least this much away to bigger and better causes than my own. To do this, I'll have to earn ten times this amount. This is the dragon I must slay. I have no doubt I can achieve this and much more.

Please don't misunderstand my point here. I'm not just trying to tell you how good I am, or how much I own. I've had my share of heartbreaks. I lost my younger brother (my only sibling) to cancer a few years ago; and one of my closest friends only last year. My mother has also had a battle with cancer. Everyone has obstacles in their lives that they must overcome. But here's the thing: if a kid from public housing can lift himself above the pack and walk through all of life's barricades and come out smiling and successful, then anybody can do it.

The question you must ask yourself is this: Am I prepared to go through ten rounds to find prosperity and happiness? To find my abundant destiny? We all have a destiny. What most people don't understand is that we choose our own destiny by the way we think. If we think poor, we get poor. If we think abundance, we get abundance.

Over the following ten rounds you'll learn about real experiences that have affected my life. These experiences have made me the person I am today. I'm hoping that my explanation of these will help you to understand that every one of us is here for a reason.

Our lives are meant to be joyous and fulfilling. We are here to prosper in every way possible.

Why would anyone choose 'poor' over 'rich'? Or 'sad' over 'happy'? Or 'sick' over 'healthy'? The only ones who would are people who don't know they actually have a choice.

I challenge you now to open your mind and let go of any 'lack of' and 'negative' thinking. Accept that what you're about to read is both true and possible. If you're ready for change, and you're prepared to make this the 'main event' of your life, then together we'll find the fighter within you.

WORK OUT YOUR OPPONENT

In a ten-round fight, this round should be used to feel out my opponent, and to work out my opponent's strengths and weaknesses. STRAIGHT RIGHT, LEFT HOOK. Once I know these things, I can then start to work out my own fight plan. To ensure I gain the most I possibly can from each fight, I'll ensure the fight lasts for as long as possible. JAB, JAB. This will help me in later fights as I draw on the experience of earlier bouts. Round 1 is also a good round to jab and move. It's when I find out that my opponent can't really hurt me, even though he's hit me with his best shot.

In life, people often look for a quick fix to their problems. But quick fixes create quick new problems. The message here is simple: Rome wasn't built in a day. In Round 1 you need to take the time to work out what the opponent to your happiness is. Is it your finances, or lack of finances? Is it your health? Your love life? Your business life? Maybe you have too much stress? Or not enough self-confidence? Is it your current weight?

Whatever the obstacle or obstacles are, you have created them. You may find this hard to believe, but they're usually only in your mind. The great news is that because you created them, you can release them from your life quite easily.

You see, what you think about is what you attract. Let me explain.

The Universal Law of Attraction says that whatever is in your life now, you have attracted. You may not have intentionally decided to repel love or money or happiness from your life, but if you spend time thinking about how bad things are you'll attract more of the same – bad relationships, financial insecurity and unhappiness.

Identify what you are thinking in terms of 'lack of', and start to think about it in an abundant way. If you don't have enough money, don't think to yourself, 'I never have enough money.' Think to yourself, 'I have more money than I know what to do with.'

I know this is difficult, and we're only in Round 1, but if you can master your thinking, you can master your life. It's just a matter of understanding that what you put in determines what comes out. Over the next ten rounds you'll learn not only the techniques, but the importance of keeping your mind filled with beautiful, uplifting thoughts, rather than ugly, sad ones. It really is that simple.

Napoleon Hill, author of *Think and Grow Rich*, said, 'Whatever the mind can conceive and believe; the mind can achieve.'

I know this concept may seem a bit alien to you at first, but by Round 10 you'll be amazed at the simplicity and effectiveness of this way of thinking. The most important thing for you to know is that you have total control over the way you think, and therefore over your life. Once you accept this is true and take responsibility for your life, you will realise that if you change your thinking to that of abundance and plenty, rather than 'lack of', your whole world will change for the better.

There is no limit to how much money you can have, or how much weight you can lose, or how great your love life can be, or how many sales you can make. You just need to see it in your mind. If you hold on to this positive, winning image, the Law of Attraction says 'and so you shall have it'.

Over the last few years I've learned from many great teachers. One of these is Dr Michael Beckwith, who taught me this: 'See what you describe, don't describe what you see.'

What he means is that most people just talk about what they see on the news and in their lives, which means they continue to get more of the same. Every day our lives are bombarded by all forms of media showing us every bad thing that has happened. And we're inundated by the complaints of our friends and acquaintances.

However, when you 'See what you describe', you get to determine what your life becomes. You describe (start a journal – write it down) what you want, then you see it in your mind. Once your conscious mind has the image firmly, confidently instilled, it tells your sub-conscious mind to bring these thoughts to action.

The best thing about your sub-conscious mind is that it only has a one-word vocabulary . . . YES. No matter what you tell it, the answer is always the same . . . YES.

You see, the sub-conscious mind is simply the vehicle used by the conscious mind to let the body know that it's made a decision. I think of it like this: the conscious mind says, 'I've made a decision, let the body know.' And the sub-conscious mind says, 'Yes.' The sub-conscious mind never actually thinks for itself. It just carries out the orders of the conscious mind.

So when your sub-conscious mind sends these signals out to the Universe, the Law of Attraction kicks in, and all of a sudden you have what you described.

We're close to the bell that ends Round 1, so take a few deep breaths and sit and think for a moment, and work out whom your opponent is.

If you're trying to lose weight, it's not the chocolate in your fridge. If you don't have enough money, it's not the poorly paid job you have. If your love life is bad, it's not your partner's fault.

The biggest obstacle between you and a life of plenitude and happiness . . . is YOU.

If a person will advance confidently in the direction of their dream and endeavour to live the life they have imagined, they will meet with success unexpected in common hours.

Henry David Thoreau

FIGHTING TIPS

Shadow boxing

One of the best ways for a fighter to keep fit, to work out his reach, and to slip his opponent's punches, is to shadow box. I would always finish up a hard day's training with a couple of rounds of shadow boxing. It helped me to loosen up my muscles, freshen up my mind and think about upcoming fights, and give my legs the stamina they were going to need in these fights. When I look back now, I realise what a great lesson in life this was, even though I didn't know it at the time.

The opponent I was shadow boxing was me. I now know that if I can overcome this opponent in life, the biggest opponent I'll ever face, I can have anything I want.

My only limitation is my own mind. Had I known this when I was fighting, I'm certain I would have gone further.

THE FIGHTER WITHIN

You see, I always thought the person that I was fighting was the person I needed to overcome. But in reality it was me, and the limitations I placed on myself, in my own mind. When you can remove the limitations that you carry in your mind, your life will become one that is truly worth living.

The next time you can't work out who your opponent is, I want you to go out into your own backyard, or outside to a quiet place in the sun, make sure that you're casting a shadow, and start shadow boxing with yourself. Throw some good punches at that shadow of yours.

Firstly it will make you smile, and when you're smiling, you're vibrating at a higher level. Then it will make you angry, because no matter how many times you hit that shadow, it just won't go down.

When you realise that the opponent you're trying to knock down is you, you'll know that the battle you have with yourself is a battle you can never win.

If you can change the way you think and remove from your mind the limitations you have on yourself, you will never have to fight *you* again.

ROUND 2

FOCUS ON WINNING

Now that I know my opponent can't hurt me, Round 2 is when I focus on winning. STRAIGHT RIGHT. I visualise in my mind a picture of the referee raising my arm as the victor. This puts me into a whole new space, both mentally and physically. DOUBLE JAB. I know I'll take a lot more punches and knocks before the fight is over, but I can see the reward and it's definitely worth fighting for.

So now you realise you are totally responsible for your life and that any opponent or obstacle in your way has been put there by you. It's disturbing, I know. But only what you create in your mind can you have in your life.

I recently met the magnificent Mary Morrissey. Mary, who has spent much time with the Dalai Lama, and who is now one of the world's great New Thought ministers and public speakers, told me this: 'Everything is created twice . . . first as a thought and then as a thing.' One of the great artists of all time, Michelangelo, confirmed this when he said: 'I see what I paint, then I paint what I see.'

In simple terms this means that if you can't imagine yourself being rich, you'll never be rich. If you can't imagine yourself being thin, you'll never be thin. And if you can't imagine yourself in a fulfilling relationship then you'll never be in one.

The Law of Thinking says, 'We attract only what we think or create.'

Focus on what you want. It doesn't matter how big or small your want is; you'll never have it if you don't focus on it.

When you focus on the end result in your mind, you start to feel good about yourself. Your body starts to feel good about how good your mind feels. When you think and feel good, you vibrate at a higher level, and you start to attract good things into your world.

Let me try and explain this as best I can. When you feel good, the energy in your body vibrates faster, which lifts your vibration to a higher level. Because you only attract into your life that which vibrates at the same level, the things you're attracting must also be vibrating at that same fast, high level.

When you feel bad, the energy in your body vibrates slowly, ensuring that you vibrate on a much lower level. This in turn means you only attract other things vibrating at the same low level.

If nothing else, I hope this helps you to understand just how important it is for you to 'feel' good inside, for as long and as often as you possibly can.

You see, the Law of Attraction won't decide to send you millions of dollars if you're thinking about how broke you are. Just like the Law of Gravity won't decide to stop you from hitting the ground if you fall off a building because it thinks you're a good person.

The Universal Laws don't have the capacity to make a decision. They just follow the Laws without emotion or discussion. However, you are the one who can make the decision. Think abundantly. Tell the Universe what you want and see yourself with the riches you desire and deserve.

Think about your life to now. Whenever you did well in an exam it wasn't because you focused on studying. Whenever you won that big sporting event it wasn't because you simply trained hard. Whenever you lost the most weight in the past it wasn't because you focused on what you were eating.

I'll bet while you were home studying, or up early training, or eating tasteless foods, you were saying to yourself: 'Oh, I hate this.'

Of course you were, but you could picture in your mind your A-grade result, or your new trophy, or your new body, and that made it all worthwhile. You were totally focused on the result, the reward for your hard work.

When we focus on what we want and send that message out to the Universe, it can but only become.

Many famous and successful people who have known about this have achieved greatness in their lifetime. There is no better example of how to send a message out, how to believe in it without question, and how to focus with absolute precision on the result, than the story of Muhammad Ali.

One of the greatest humanitarians of all time, and also one of the greatest boxers of all time, Muhammad Ali agreed to fight the undefeated George Foreman in Zaire for the world title back in 1974. Let me try and put this into perspective. After spending three years in prison for not going to Vietnam, Muhammad Ali fought Joe Frazier for the world title and lost. Joe Frazier then fought George Foreman, who pounded him into submission by way of a second-round knockout. So Ali lost to Frazier and Frazier lost to Foreman.

Foreman was a hulk of a man, and everybody tried to talk Ali out of taking the fight. But even though there wasn't a person alive who thought he could beat Foreman, Ali accepted.

When Ali got to Zaire a few weeks before the fight, the talk in the media was that Foreman would massacre him in the ring. They said Ali was too old and that Foreman was too big. Ali trained hard, as always, and ignored the media opinion.

A couple of days before the fight, Foreman received a cut eye while sparring.

After the doctor examined the cut, promoter Don King gave the Ali camp three choices: 1. Cancel the fight 2. Go home to the USA and come back and fight in six weeks or 3. Stay in Zaire for six weeks and then fight.

The media predicted the Ali camp would take the first choice. Ali's trainers and managers all wanted to do so. They were just happy that their fighter didn't have to get hurt. But Ali decided he'd stay. He chose option 3. You see, it didn't matter to him that nobody thought he could beat Foreman. He knew he would win . . . no matter what.

Ali had already seen the fight in his own mind. He'd already sent the message out to the Universe and he knew the Law of Attraction would take care of the rest.

About a week before the fight, both fighters came together for a press conference. The media was asking questions to both fighters when one man asked them how they thought the fight would end.

Foreman answered first. He said he would knock Ali out in the first or second round. Ali answered next. He said he predicted a knockout in the eighth round.

The media joked and laughed and asked Ali if he really thought he'd last that long. They thought Ali was predicting that he'd be knocked out by Foreman in Round 8. Only Ali himself knew what he was predicting, and the rest is history.

From the second the bell sounded for Round 1, Foreman was on the attack. He smashed Ali round after round, yet Ali kept calling him on. Ali would lean back on the ropes and motion Foreman to come on. It was the discovery of his 'Rope-a-Dope' trick.

Angelo Dundee, Ali's trainer, yelled and screamed at Ali to get off the ropes and get away from Foreman.

He was afraid Ali would be seriously injured if he continued to get hit by Foreman's loaded punches. Yet Ali stayed put, taunting and teasing Foreman to come and finish him.

In the corner after the seventh round, Angelo Dundee told Ali that if he didn't stay away from Foreman he would get seriously hurt. Ali told Angelo not to worry, as everything was going to plan. Angelo yelled some more and then asked, 'Whose plan?' Ali just smiled as the bell rang for the eighth round and headed back to the centre ring.

For the first half of the round Ali was smashed around just like in the previous seven rounds. But Foreman was tiring due to the amount of punches he'd thrown, and Ali was aware of what was happening. All of sudden, Ali saw an opening and took it. He landed a brutal combination of a left hook followed by a straight right that sent Foreman crashing to the canvas.

There was never a chance that Foreman would get up. He was finished, and Ali knew it before anybody else. You see, he'd already seen the outcome in his mind.

That day, Muhammad Ali pulled off one of the greatest upsets of all time. Books and movies have been written and made about this fight. It's an almost unbelievable story. Yet to Ali, it was no surprise.

Ali's win that day was governed by the Universal Laws. Because he went after the picture he held in his mind with faith and persistence, the Law of Attraction delivered to him the outcome he desired.

The Law of Compensation says, 'You must earn what you receive or you cannot keep it.' When you look at Muhammad Ali's life up to this fight you will surely see that he earned his victory. He'd spent three years in jail because of his religious beliefs for refusing to go to war in Vietnam. He also had his jaw broken in a fifteen-round fight with Joe Frazier. Later in his career, Ali went on to become the first man in history to win the World Heavyweight Title three times, when he defeated the much younger Leon Spinks. The Law of Compensation played an integral part throughout the career of possibly the greatest boxer the world has ever seen.

If you want success in your life, you must alter the way you think. When you focus on what you want and where you want to be in life with conviction and motivation, it will always be. Never take your focus off the end result, the reward. Keep it there, and obstacles and opponents will move aside or disappear, and you won't even know why. You don't need to know why.

Focus on what you want and how you want your life to be, and the Universe will do the rest.

FOCUS.
It's easy to focus if you write down what you want. For example:
- I will lose 10 kilos in three months.

- I will have a job that pays me $200,000 a year within the next twelve months.
- I will be living in a $2 million home.
- I will live in a fulfilling, loving relationship.
- I will live my life in a disease-free and healthy body.

Be sure that what you write down is believable to you, and know that what you continue to focus on will be attracted to you. If you accept this, you'll understand how damaging thoughts of 'not enough money' or 'how bad my job is' or 'my relationship sucks' are to your results and rewards.

Focus on winning and let the rest take care of itself. You'll be healthier, happier, more prosperous, more loving and, above all, on your way to a life of wealth and abundance.

Don't be afraid of success and ensure that the success you choose for yourself is worthy of YOU. Dream big!

Desire backed by faith knows no such word as impossible.

Napoleon Hill

FIGHTING TIPS

Finding that place

When I was boxing, I used to train hard. I'd work out at the gym five days a week, and I'd run seven days a week. Not to mention the constant dieting to make the weight. It's hard to keep motivated to train like this, so what I used to do was put myself into a good frame of mind, and when I did this, I found I could always get through.

I would picture myself getting into the ring on fight night with hundreds of my friends cheering for me. The feeling was exhilarating. This wasn't just any fight, though, it was a title fight, and the prize was a big leather belt.

I'd picture myself knocking out my opponent, and then the referee placing the gold-laden belt around my waist.

After just two years of boxing, or should I say after just

two years of visualising myself as the champion, I won a New South Wales Featherweight title.

I remember feeling so proud and so thankful to my trainer, who'd spent so much time getting me there. But I also remember not feeling surprised. I knew I'd already been there and won the title, even if it was only in my mind.

Of course, I didn't know anything about the Laws of Attraction back then. It's only now that I understand how these Laws have affected my life.

Now, when I'm in a place that I really don't want to be in, because it drains me, or because it makes me sad or because it makes me worry, I think about how relaxed and grateful I feel when I'm at my holiday home at Sanctuary Cove. When I feel this good my vibration moves to a higher level, which means I attract better things into my life. I'm also much more creative when my vibration is high.

When you're feeling down, think about a place in your mind that makes you feel good. Maybe it was a night out with a loved one, or maybe it was your last holiday, or maybe it was the feeling you had when you moved into your new home. Whatever it is, find it and hold it in your mind until your vibration lifts. Very soon, instead of feeling down you'll start to feel up. And the more you think about that 'good' time in your life, the more up you'll feel.

It's the same when you're visualising how your life will be in the future. You imagine yourself with a great deal of money, or with a new romantic partner, or at your new perfect weight, and it makes you feel good.

FOCUS ON WINNING

The longer you can hold that image in your mind, the longer you'll be feeling good, and the sooner the Law of Attraction will bring this image into reality.

OVERCOME THE OBSTACLES

Round 3 is when I need to overcome the obstacles of winning. JAB, JAB. I now know my opponent can't really hurt me and I've seen myself as the winner. But this is where the 'what ifs' start to show up. STRAIGHT RIGHT. What if he catches me with a big left hook that I'm not ready for? What if I'm not fit enough to go the rounds? Did I train hard enough? What if I forget what I've been taught? BOB AND WEAVE. If I can just get through this round, I know the rest of the fight will fall into place. I need to convince myself right now that yes, I am fit enough, and that I have trained hard enough, and that I won't forget what I've been taught.

This is where most people get a reality check. You start to share what you've learned with family and friends and they start saying things like, 'Do you really think this is right for you?', or, 'I've seen all this stuff before, it doesn't work', or, 'I tried that, it's no good.' Because you respect and love these people, you listen to what they say. Unfortunately, it affects the way YOU think, which in turn affects what YOU do.

You start to question yourself, and all of a sudden you're back where you started.

Hang up the phone! I've learned in my life, especially my boxing life, that everyone's an expert. They all know better than you do, even though they've never had a fight. Make the decision to spend less time with these friends and more time with like-minded people who are also looking to grow their life experience.

You're reading this book because you want to improve your life in some way, shape or form. Here's the thing: you've already seen the winning picture of you in your mind. You're halfway there. The only 'real' obstacles you'll ever come across are negative people.

Of course, there are other obstacles you'll face at some stage in your life – like not enough sales, too much weight, poor health, an unhappy relationship, or not enough money. The same theory applies: spend less time with junk food, spend less time with bad people, spend less time thinking about poor health and less time worrying about not enough money. These too can be overcome if you focus on the reward, rather than on the problem.

There are some Fighting Tips at the end of Round 6 that will teach you all about The Gallery of Good and Evil. Practise this method and you will never have to worry about the obstacles in your life again.

I've been privileged to have seen many great public speakers throughout my life. Some specialise in 'sharing their knowledge'. Others focus on 'calling to action'. When I look back on what I've heard and learned, nobody has impressed me with his story-telling ability as much as Doug Wead.

Former advisor to the US government, Doug Wead, is now regarded as one of the best motivational speakers on the planet. At a seminar I attended in Mexico, Doug told a story about David and the Princess. He said, 'I know you know it, it's the Bible story about when David kills the giant.' His version goes like this:

The Israelites and the Philistines stood on opposite sides of a riverbed ready to do battle. Both armies were many thousands strong. Rather than lose thousands of lives in battle, the Philistines sent their biggest fighter forward, along with a message to the Israelites that if one of them could defeat this man, Goliath, they would accept defeat and go on home.

To the astonishment of the Philistines, every Israelite turned and ran. Not one of them believed that Goliath could be beaten.

Back at the Israelite village, the King visited his terrified soldiers and told them that if there was an Israelite among them who could defeat the Philistine fighter, Goliath, he would win the hand of the King's daughter in marriage.

When David arrived back at the village, he overheard some soldiers talking about the Princess. He hadn't heard the King's offer in person, so he interrupted and asked, 'Did you say that the man who slays the giant Goliath gets the hand of the Princess in marriage?'

The soldiers replied that this was true, and added that the Princess bathed in a holy soap that left her skin sweet-smelling and soft.

David asked again: 'The reward for the man who slays Goliath is the hand of the Princess?'

Again, the soldiers confirmed that this was true.

That night at home, David overhead his brothers talking about the Princess. He asked them again about the reward for slaying the giant and they confirmed that it was indeed the hand of the Princess.

David then told his brothers that he would slay the giant and win the hand of the Princess. His brothers laughed and said, 'You couldn't slay the giant; you're just a small peasant boy.'

All night David dreamed about what it would be like to be married to the Princess, how soft she would feel and how sweet she would smell. He pictured himself feeding her and holding her in his arms, and he imagined that she would adore him just as much as he adored her.

The next day David went back to the riverbed where the Philistines waited. Goliath was still at the front, calling for a challenger.

I'm sure you know what happened next. David, with his slingshot, slew the giant Goliath and won the hand of the Princess. And he lived happily ever after.

The message in this story is simple. David didn't focus on Goliath, he focused on the Princess.

When you take your focus off the obstacles in your life and focus only on the reward, you will achieve great success.

Hold that winning picture in your mind with clarity and confidence, and the obstacles in your life will become so insignificant that you won't see them or think about them again.

Dr Michael Beckwith says it like this: 'If you

can hold it in your head, you can hold it in your hand.' Believe in yourself and take your focus off the obstacles, whatever they are, and you will be one step closer to your dreams.

The road to success is lined with many tempting parking spaces.

Unknown

FIGHTING TIPS

The Stick Figure

Dr Thurman Fleet designed the 'Stick Figure' concept in the 1930s. Bob Proctor, best-selling author of *You Were Born Rich* and master teacher of the power of the mind, embraced this concept in his teachings and has passed it on to his protégé and partner, Paul Martinelli, President of Life-Success Consulting. A highly sought-after public speaker and teacher of the Universal Laws, Paul describes this concept as well as anyone I know. I'll use Paul's explanation in the hope that you understand it in the same way I did.

The stick figure represents your mind and your body. Notice that the mind is so much larger than the body. This is because the mind has so much more influence over your life than the body does.

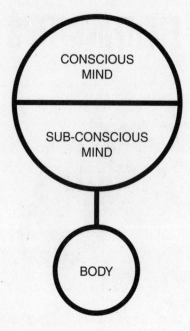

Let's work from the top down.

THE CONSCIOUS MIND: This is where your decisions are made. Through your conscious mind, you choose the things you want in your life. Your conscious mind has the option to accept or reject what is put before it. It can also originate ideas and create new thoughts and images. The conscious mind is fed information by way of your senses: sight, sound, smell, taste and touch. If you're not thinking, and using your conscious mind as a filter, it will send whatever it is taking in directly to your sub-conscious mind.

THE SUB-CONSCIOUS MIND: Based on the information sent to it by the conscious mind, the sub-conscious mind turns these thoughts into feelings which sets up a vibration, turning your feelings into action. For example, the conscious mind takes in the news of the day and is feeling very down. It then sends a message to the sub-conscious mind that says, 'I'm feeling down.' And because we know that the sub-conscious mind has only a one-word vocabulary, it replies the only way it knows how . . . YES.

The sub-conscious mind then sends this 'negative' vibration to the body, which is programmed to act on the vibrations of the sub-conscious mind.

Of course, if the conscious mind has been thinking about the abundance of good that is about to come into its life, it will send a signal to the sub-conscious mind that says, 'I'm feeling great', to which the sub-conscious mind will reply . . . YES.

The sub-conscious mind will then send a 'positive' vibration to the body and, of course, the body will act on this vibration accordingly.

THE BODY turns thoughts and feelings impressed upon the sub-conscious mind into action.

This may take a little while to understand, but when you do it will make perfect sense. The only thing we have control over is our conscious mind. What we choose to put in our sub-conscious mind determines how we feel, which in turn determines how we act. If we choose to put doom and gloom and sad and ugly information into our conscious mind, the message we're sending to our body through our sub-conscious mind is the same.

If we choose to put beauty and abundance and success and greatness in, our actions will mimic these thoughts.

Simply put, we CHOOSE what goes into our conscious mind. Our conscious mind CAUSES the feelings in our sub-conscious mind. Our sub-conscious mind CAUSES the action of our body.

Once you accept that this is the Law, you become much more careful about what you put into your conscious mind. Feed it with love and abundant thinking and it will flourish and send only 'good' messages to your sub-conscious mind.

When the vibrations sent from your sub-conscious mind to your body are based on only 'good' feelings, you will start to attract only 'good' things into your life.

LOOK FOR OPENINGS

Round 4 is a good round. RIGHT CROSS. I know I can't be hurt (well, not too badly), I'm focused, and now I need to look for openings. Does he drop his right hand when he throws his left? LEFT HOOK. Does he leave himself open when he goes under my punches? Is his stomach his weakest spot? LEFT RIP. Is he fit enough to keep up the pace? These are all opportunities on which to capitalise. I need to find these openings, I know they exist, and I will take advantage then and there. I won't wait.

Far too often, people do all the right things to create opportunities in their lives, yet when these opportunities appear, they fail to capitalise on them.

When you know who your opponent is (you) and you're focused on winning (you can see the picture in your mind) and you've overcome the obstacles (negative friends and family), good things will start to happen.

You need to recognise these openings and take advantage of them. Immediately.

If you don't grab an opportunity and run with it, you'll miss out. Later on you'll say, 'Oh yeah, I had a chance to do that but I wasn't quite sure at the time.'

Opportunities and openings appear at the most unexpected of times. And because they're so unexpected, most people don't see them. I know people who have seized the moment, found an opening and taken advantage of it. They've then gone on to be rich or famous beyond belief.

Yet others I've met have told me how they regret not capitalising on an opportunity that had presented itself because they didn't realise it was an opening, or because they really weren't ready at the time.

I'm sure you've known people who have had the same experiences. And whether they took the opening or they didn't, every one of them had a story to tell.

A couple of years ago, following the devastation of the New Orleans flood, I heard a terrific story.

The story went like this:

Tom was a religious man, a servant to God his entire life. As the waters rose around the house in which Tom lived, all of the neighbours evacuated. Tom decided he'd stay put and let the Lord look after him.

As the tide rose to the bottom of the windows in Tom's house, he stood at the front door and praised the Lord. Almost everyone else around had fled.

A double-decker bus was passing, taking others to safety, when the driver saw Tom and called out, 'Tom, get in, I'll drive you to safety.'

Tom refused and cried out, 'The Lord will take care of me.'

Half an hour later, as the water level covered the first floor of Tom's house, a man in a rowboat was passing when he saw Tom peering through the windows on the second level. 'Tom,' the man yelled, 'swim out to me and I'll take you to safety.'

Once again, Tom refused. He yelled back to the man in the boat, 'The Lord will take care of me.'

As the waters rose to the roof level of his home, Tom scrambled onto his roof and began praying. At this time a helicopter flying others to safety saw Tom and hovered above his house. The pilot dropped a rope ladder down to near where Tom was sitting and yelled to Tom, 'Climb up the ladder and I'll fly you to safety.'

Of course, Tom's faith stood strong and he yelled back to the pilot, 'Thank you, but no. The Lord will take care of me.'

Less than an hour later the whole neighbourhood was under water. Tom drowned that day, but as his faith predicted, he ended up in heaven. As soon as he arrived, he demanded an audience with God.

When God had finished his meetings for the day he summoned Tom to his chambers. As soon as Tom arrived he said to God, 'Lord, you know I've been a faithful servant of yours for my entire life?'

'Yes, I know this, Tom,' God replied.

'And you know I've spread the word of love and peace and of God ever since I was able,' Tom continued.

'Yes, Tom, I know this.'

'And you know, Lord, that I've never asked you for anything in my entire life?'

'Yes, Tom, I know this.'

A little frustrated, Tom continued, 'Well, Lord, if you know all of this, why didn't you save me the first time I ever needed your help?'

God looked at Tom and raised his arms in the air, then said, 'Well, Tom, I sent you a bus, a boat and a helicopter, how much more could I do?'

The point here is this: whether you have faith in God, the spirit, the Universe, or whoever, your higher power can only do so much. At some stage it has to hand the creative power over to you. You need to be aware of that on which you focus, because once you're in sync with the Universe, once you actually connect through the picture you hold in your mind, there is no stopping the abundance that will enter your life. You will have more money than you need, more love, more sales, greater weight loss and better results in life than you could ever have imagined.

Remember the saying, 'Be careful what you wish for.' The reason I tell you this is because I know, from personal experience, that you can have anything and everything you wish for and a whole lot more, if you focus on winning and take advantage of the openings as they present themselves.

The Laws of the Universe are powerful, and when you understand that they exist and invite them into your life, you will have unlimited creative ability to design the life you want, rather than to live in the life you don't.

LOOK FOR OPENINGS

The Law of Supply says that abundance is already there. It comes from one source (the Universe) but through many different channels. You need to ensure that you are plugged in to as many of these channels as possible.

Know that you can have anything that you want as long as you're prepared to take action. Look for the openings.

We all walk in the dark and each of us must learn to turn on his or her own light.

Earl Nightingale

FIGHTING TIPS

The more you help others . . .

'The more you help others, the more they help you.' You've probably heard this saying a hundred times or more throughout your life. Every religion teaches it, every charity practises it, and your mother would have said it to you dozens of times as you were growing up.

Well, here's the thing . . . it actually works. It's based on the Universal Law of Giving that says, 'As you freely give so shall you freely receive.' And it's not just to do with money or possessions.

Let me give you an example. When I first started boxing I was used as a sparring partner by fighters who had many more fights and much more experience than me.

Sometimes these fighters, instead of using me to improve their fitness and teaching me the art of boxing, decided that I should be used solely as a punching bag. Being such a novice, it was obvious that I couldn't hurt them, so they'd just slug off on me, proving to anyone watching how good they were.

As I had more fights and started to improve my skills, I too had the opportunity of sparring with less experienced fighters. Not once did I try to intentionally hurt an opponent. Not once did I try to show others how good I was by belting a novice.

Instead, I used the partners to improve my stamina and my defensive skills, and to teach them the art of boxing. After all, they were doing me a favour by sparring with me.

As experienced fighters get older, inexperienced fighters get better. Some years later, at a time when I was at the peak of my career, I had the opportunity of sparring again with some of the fighters who had used me as their punching bag when I had first learned the trade.

These fighters were now well past their prime. They were older and slower, and after these later bouts I knew there wasn't one of them who didn't wish they'd been just a little kinder, and shown a little more humility, and been just a little more giving, when we'd sparred all those years ago.

I was lucky enough never to have this same problem with the fighters I'd sparred with earlier in their careers, and it was for two reasons. Firstly, when the younger fighters sparred with me later in their careers, they never had a reason to get back at me; and secondly, I retired while I was still on top.

I won my last two fights and decided I'd done enough. Unlike 97 per cent of all fighters, I retired on a win.

'The more you help others, the more they help you' is so true in every aspect of life, and because it's based on the Law of Giving it can't help but come true, every time.

Once you become fully aware of this Law, you will constantly see the results of it around you. While I like to think of myself as a generous person, sometimes I forget about the Law of Giving. I'll do something to help improve someone else's life, and a week or two later, something good happens to me.

Now, my life constantly brings me many rewards. But I always attribute these rewards to my continual usage of the Law of Attraction. I sometimes forget that they are also sent to me because of the Law of Giving.

Let me give you some real examples of how the Law of Giving actually works:

1. As a boss I always try to look after my staff, paying them well and spoiling them in different ways; and allowing them time off work when they need it. There came a time when one of our major funders called us on a Thursday and said, 'Hey, we'll be out to do an audit on your files tomorrow.' Now, when you have an audit done, you need to make sure that every file is in perfect order, that everything is where it should be, and that all of the loan information is easily accessible. With hundreds of files that may be audited, the staff members got straight to work. They set up tables all over the office, and started to go through the files individually, ensuring that when

the auditors picked up each file, it would be easy for them to do their job. Some of the staff normally finished their workday at 4 pm. Others at 5 pm. We ordered in pizzas for dinner and at 11 pm we were all still working as a team, to get through every file and ensure it was in perfect order. My staff don't get paid overtime. They're all on salaries. The next day, the auditors came in, spent a few hours reviewing our files, and then told us how beautifully they were kept.

2. A friend of mine is a personal fitness trainer who goes out of his way to help his clients to lose weight and to achieve their personal fitness goals, yet he never charges more than the standard training fee. His clients invariably reach their perfect weights and their fitness goals, then proceed to tell everyone they know about their trainer, who in turn picks up dozens of new clients without spending a cent on advertising.

3. Another friend of mine is a doctor, who told me this story about a colleague of his, a world-renowned heart specialist. This heart specialist always taught his interns everything there was to know about the heart, and everything he had ever learned from the hundreds of operations he'd performed. He would never leave anything out of his teachings. Although he was ageing, he'd spend countless 'extra' hours with his protégées, so that one day they would be just like him . . . saving lives on a regular basis.

One night, the mentor had a massive heart attack and was rushed to hospital with little hope of surviving.

One of his students, who had been under the doctor's tutelage for the past ten years, was called in to perform the operation. It took the student twelve long hours and he had to call on everything he'd ever been taught by his amazing mentor. Unsurprisingly, the operation was a success. The mentor recovered fully and went on to save many more lives.

There's one more example I'd like to share with you, and it only happened while writing this book. I was purchasing some sushi in a large food court in Sydney on a Sunday afternoon. As I was about to walk away, I noticed a mobile phone sitting on the silver bench on the customer side of the counter. It looked like a new model, so I picked it up and thought about handing it over to the young lady who'd just served me, but then decided that to ensure it got back to its rightful owner, I should return it myself.

I had a quick look through the address book and noticed a name: 'Andre Boyfriend'. I called the number and proceeded to tell Andre that I'd found a phone and that his name was in the address book listed under 'Andre Boyfriend'.

He thought for a minute, and then said, 'Oh, I think that might be my girlfriend's mother's phone.' I suggested that his girlfriend's mother give me a call and we'd work out how to get the phone back to her.

A few minutes later, the phone rang and it was Andre's girlfriend, Aggy, who informed me that her mother had lost her phone and was certain she'd never see it again. She said her mum had paid $1000 for the phone a week earlier.

The next day, Monday, Aggy's mum and I met up. She

came to my office, and couldn't have been more appre-
ciative. Her name was Silvia, and she had a little gift of
beautiful homemade cakes as a 'thank you' for returning
her phone.

I thanked her for the cakes but said they weren't neces-
sary and that she should keep them. I then told her that
when I had seen her phone sitting there on the counter, I'd
thought about how inconvenient it would be for me if I'd lost
my phone, and thus that was the reason I picked it up.

Aggy's mum had a little chuckle and then said to me, 'You
know, this is so strange. I was at a restaurant on Saturday
evening, and as I was leaving I noticed a wallet on the table
next to me. I picked it up and checked inside, and apart
from a number of credit cards and a driver's licence, there
was just over $700 in cash. I thought about giving it to the
waiter, but then decided that it would probably be better if I
returned it myself. When I arrived home that night, I looked
through the phone book and found a local number for the
name on the driver's licence. I then called Ron and told him
that I'd found his wallet at the restaurant.

'The owner, Ron, was ecstatic. He said when he'd arrived
home he'd realised he didn't have his wallet. After checking
through his car, and then phoning the restaurant, he thought
he'd lost it for good. He told me he'd just withdrawn $800
out of his account from a cash machine as he was taking a
friend to dinner. He said his friend had done some repairs
on his car and wouldn't take any money for the work, so he
wanted to thank him.

'On Sunday morning, Ron came around to my house

and collected his wallet. He offered me $200 of the cash as a reward. I rejected it and told Ron that if I lost my wallet, I would hope that somebody would return it to me. I told him it would bring me good karma. And guess what . . . within a matter of hours, it did.'

Now I have to tell you, when Silvia told me this story, the hairs on the back of my neck (not that there are many) stood up. Before she left my office, I gave Silvia a big hug and told her she was a good lady, and that if more people thought and acted the way she did, the world would be an even better place to live.

While reflecting on this beautiful episode and devouring another mouthful of the homemade cakes that Silvia had left for me (I'd tried to give them back – she wouldn't take them), it suddenly dawned on me that this was just another example of how the Universal Laws affect our lives. I know some will say 'it's just a coincidence', and others may say 'that's a load of crap', but to those people I say this: 'Try it, and see what happens.' You have nothing to lose by giving your time, knowledge, kindness, love, gratitude or praise to others. Why not just go ahead and do it, and see for yourself what kind of results it brings to your life.

We accept that the Law of Gravity is real. And we live within its rules or we get hurt. We also accept that the Law of Nature is real. It never fails. The sun shines every day. When it rains, plants grow, grass grows, trees grow, weeds grow, food grows.

We rely on the Law of Nature to be successful. Dogs give birth to puppies, lions give birth to lion cubs, and monkeys give birth to baby monkeys. We couldn't survive if this wasn't the case. How could we plan for future generations?

When we plant corn seeds we get corn. When we plant potato seeds we get potatoes. Imagine what would happen if we planted rice seeds and we grew pineapples? We would have no way of controlling our food supply. More people would starve.

If we accept that these Laws truly exist, why is it so hard to imagine that the Universe has other Laws that affect our lives? Like the Law of Giving?

Ron took his friend to dinner and got his wallet back. Silvia gave Ron his wallet back and got her mobile phone back. Rocky gave Silvia her phone back and got some delicious cakes. This is how it works. It makes sense, doesn't it?

When you can help others without the expectation of remuneration or payback, you are in alignment with the Law of Giving. And when you live your life by way of the Laws of the Universe, you will find harmony and peace within your inner self.

The more you help others, the better your own life will become.

DIG DEEP

Round 5 is one of the hardest rounds of the fight, as this is the round where I find out what's inside me. RIGHT TO THE BODY. I'm almost halfway, I know I'm ahead on points, but I'm tired and aching from the amount of punishment I've absorbed. The finish line seems so far away and I start to doubt my own ability to go the distance. BOB AND WEAVE. This is the time I need to dig deep and ask myself who I really am.

Many people call this 'the crossroads' of their lives. We've all been there. It's the point in our journey where we get to decide which way to go, forward or back. And this really is the only choice. Do I continue forward on the same path with the knowledge I've gained, and continue to explore the unknown? Or do I turn around and go back to my 'safe' life of being average?

Although the following numbers are not set in concrete, from the countless books and articles I've read, and from the many seminars I've attended, it appears that around 95 per cent of people who reach this crossroad turn back, afraid of the unknown. The really amazing thing about the 5 per cent or so of people who go forward, is that to them there is no unknown. You see, they've already visualised what their future life will become. They know what to expect . . . they've already seen it.

The truth is, it's much easier to go back. That's why most people go back. To go forward you really need to go deep inside yourself, to dig deep, and to ask yourself some important questions about your dreams.

These are the questions that Mary Morrissey made me ask myself:

1. Does my dream give me life?
2. Will my dream require that I grow?
3. Does it align with my core values?
4. Do I need help from a higher power?
5. Is there some good in this dream for others?

Most people will answer the first three questions with a resounding YES. It's the next two questions they have trouble with. I was one of these people. I couldn't imagine myself needing help from a higher power. And my idea about making money was to improve MY lifestyle.

What I now realise is that there is a higher power, and that the ultimate motive of wealth is to be able to give it away.

Bill Gates, one of the wealthiest people alive, gives away hundreds of millions of dollars to charities every year. The more Bill gives away, the more money he makes. You see, he understands the Law of Giving, although in his commercial world it would be referred to as the Law of Economics. The Law of Economics neither recognises nor tolerates getting without giving, for long.

My understanding of this is that if one gives, one must surely get. And the more one gives, the more one must get.

This is almost the same principal as the Law of Giving. You may have heard people say 'what goes around comes around' or 'the more you give the more you get'. Both of these sayings are loosely based on the same Law. When you understand and accept that these Laws exist, you too will be able to answer yes to all five of Mary's questions.

I recently met a young guy on a cruise who told me his amazing story. His name was Danny, and he had a scar on his chin and what looked like burn marks on his neck. Being the inquisitive person that I am, I asked him how they got there.

This is my recollection of what Danny told me.

'I'd been feeling down and depressed for some time. Things just weren't going well in my life. I needed to feel good so I went for a ride on my motorbike. When I ride my bike I forget all about the rest of my life. And the faster I go, the more I forget.

'This day I was really speeding along. I don't remember how fast I was going, but it felt like 150 km/h. I was approaching an intersection on the inside lane when a van turned in front of me. I tried to brake but I was going too fast, and I knew I was in for a bang.

'Well, I was right. I hit the side of the van at speed and crashed into the back window before being catapulted more than ten metres in the air, over the top of the traffic lights. I then came crashing back down to earth and landed flush on my chin.

'Now, at this stage my memory fades a little, but I was still conscious. I can remember the ambulance guys talking about me; in fact, I can still remember what they looked like.

'Anyway, when I hit the ground my jaw cracked, leaving a gap a couple of centimetres wide. Some teeth just popped straight out. My helmet smashed in two, and my neck, which had been almost severed by the window on the way up, was bleeding badly. I severed three veins in my neck, including the jugular, as well as all the arteries and muscles on the left side. I smashed my knee and split my tibia, my left hand was crushed, and I dislocated my shoulder and fractured my neck.

'I also lost four litres of blood. The ambos later told me that they had to lift my head forward to see if it was still attached to my body. Thankfully, it was.

'The good thing was I was still alive. In the hospital they patched me up as best they could. I was in a coma for two weeks. During this time, they told my mum that if I made it, I'd probably be a vegetable, and even if I wasn't, I'd never walk or talk again.

'Not long after I regained consciousness, the doctors declared that my brain was intact. My body wasn't so good, and the only thing I could move was my right arm. This was a start.

'I needed constant 24-hour care, so my mum gave up her work and came to the hospital every day to look after me. I didn't have much money, only about $15,000 in savings, but I told my mum to live off this for as long as she could.

'So there I was in hospital, my mind getting stronger and my mum by my side. I started to think about my future, the one the doctors continued to tell my mother I would have, confined to a wheelchair. This wasn't sounding too appealing to me – oh, and did I mention that my fiancée decided to leave me? Well, she did.

'Needless to say, I wasn't feeling too good about anything, but I knew I was a fighter, and I was determined to prove the doctors wrong.

'It was about this time that my friends who were visiting me in hospital started to tell me about a movie they'd seen that related to the Law of Attraction. They said I reminded them of the miracle man in the movie. I had my mum do some research on the Law of Attraction, and I was so inspired by what I was reading and seeing, I knew then and there that the doctors were wrong.

'I remember the day my mum came to the hospital and I pointed with my only working limb, my right arm, to the little toe on my left foot. It was actually moving, only slightly, but it was moving.

'Over the next few months I continued to get stronger and more muscles were coming back to life. They didn't really have a choice as my mind and I were collaborating, and we both knew it was only a matter of time.

'The day I left hospital was the first time I'd actually walked since the accident. I walked out pushing the wheelchair one of the nurses had left beside my bed for me to be wheeled out in. I know I amazed a lot of doctors and nurses that day.'

It was now two years later, and after 12 months in hospital and another 12 months of painful physiotherapy and facial reconstruction, Danny appeared to be almost fully recovered. He told me he'd recently been back on his motorbike, although not yet on the road. He also told me of his vision to share his story with others, especially the doctors who had all but written him off.

I saw Danny again 24 hours later and he told me he'd just been booked to speak at a conference in Los Angeles, and also that he'd been offered a free position on a $20,000 professional speaking course. He was ecstatic as he told me, and I knew then and there that Danny's life was just beginning.

There are beautiful stories like Danny's surfacing every day. They're not all so gruesome and not all so inspiring, but they all have one thing in common . . .

they're all about normal people who reach a crossroad in their lives, and make a decision to go forward.

When you reach the crossroad in your life, dig deep, go forward, and let the Universe take care of the rest.

The greatest danger for most of us is not that we aim too high and we miss it, but we aim too low and reach it.

Michelangelo

FIGHTING TIPS

The bus ride back

Here's what I've found: it doesn't matter how positive your attitude is, or how much success you've achieved in your life, there will always be 'down' times. And when your life is based on the principles in this book, utilising the Laws of the Universe, those 'down' times will feel so far away from the heights on which you will normally be vibrating.

So here's what I do: when I'm down, I imagine myself standing by the side of the road in the crappiest place I can think of. I'm wearing crappy clothes and I know they're not mine because they don't even fit me properly. There's always a lot of traffic on the side of the road on which I'm standing, and it's really speeding past me. If I stepped off the kerb, I'd surely be run down.

Yet on the other side of the road there is no traffic, just buses, red buses, lined up at the kerb, like the ones you see at San Diego airport. There are so many buses that they're almost back-to-back, and the destination on the front of every bus says 'SUCCESS'.

Now I know I'm in a 'down' state at the moment, and I know my vibration is very low, but I realise that if I can just get across to the other side of the road and jump onto one of those buses, I'll be on my way back to an 'up' state of mind.

When I look more closely across the road, I can see that there are so many red buses heading back to 'SUCCESS' that it really won't matter how long it takes me to cross the road, because there will still be a bus waiting for me when I get there.

Already my vibration starts to lift and I notice a tiny break in the speeding traffic before me. It's not much of a break, and definitely not enough to get through, but it is a break. As I imagine myself stepping onto the bus and walking past the driver, the tiny break in the traffic starts to get larger. I'm now visualising myself sitting on the bus. The driver takes off and I'm enjoying the view as we head off on-route to our destination.

After a short ride, the bus pulls into the 'SUCCESS' stop, and funnily enough, I'm now dressed in my best suit. Back at the side of the road my vibration is lifting and the break in the traffic increases even more. In fact, it appears the traffic has slowed down considerably.

From here on is where you get creative with YOUR dreams. But, for the record, here are mine.

DIG DEEP

I walk from the 'SUCCESS' stop and jump into my red Ferrari (I have to dream too). I drive off with the top down and the music playing loudly. I can see myself singing along; boy, it's a beautiful day outside. I imagine walking into my city office and admiring the views of the city and harbour. My personal assistant (who just happens to look like Cindy Crawford) sits a freshly brewed skinny cappuccino on my desk and reminds me of the dinner reservation with my children tonight. I pick up the phone and it's my girlfriend, who says she can't wait to see me, that she just bought a new dress, and that she loves me.

I open my mail and there's a postcard from my mother. On the front is a picture of the coast of Mexico and on the back is written, '*We're having a wonderful time on the cruise, wish you were here. Thanks again for such a wonderful gift.*'

I now go online to check out my personal bank account balance, and yep, it's even more than when I last checked: $10,565,300.67. How blessed am I?

And best of all, I haven't even stepped off the kerb yet. I'm still back at the side of the road and the traffic in front of me is almost stationary. I step off the kerb and walk easily across the road. As I step on to the next red bus, the driver asks, 'How's your day been, sir?' To which I reply, 'Couldn't be better.'

You see, even though the physical reality of my life may be in a 'down' place, my mind will always have the power to lift me back to success. I can create in my mind whatever my idea of success is, with no limits and no boundaries.

And if I can focus on my success with desire, and faith, and persistence, I can have that success, whatever it is, in my physical life.

And you can too. Ensure that YOUR dreams of success are big ones. Only then will you have first-hand proof that the Laws of the Universe are greater than anyone could possibly imagine.

WEATHER THE STORM

In Round 6, I know that I'm closer to the finish line than I am to the start. RIGHT CROSS. My opponent realises that he's behind and he'll come back fighting with everything he has. My opponent knows that if he can win every round from hereon in, he's still got a chance of winning the fight. STRAIGHT LEFT, LEFT HOOK. A good fighter needs to weather the storm, and that's exactly what I'll do. I'll go back to basics and continue on with the fight plan with which I started the fight. MOVE. I need to keep a clear head and hold firmly in my mind the picture of the referee raising my arm at the end of the fight.

You've made the decision to go forward, yet the obstacles continue to niggle away at you. You've used up a lot of energy by digging deep and you're now at your most vulnerable.

Your family and friends are checking in to see that you're doing okay, and that you've finally dropped those silly ideas of being successful.

For those of you trying to lose weight, a KFC has just opened up around the corner from where you live.

For those of you looking to have millions of dollars, your bank balance is down to just a few hundred.

For sales people, your biggest client just found a cheaper product than yours.

You're up to your neck in obstacles and you're tired, almost exhausted. This is the time you need to weather the storm.

You see, once you're past this hurdle the rest is easy.

By ignoring the obstacles and focusing on the reward again, you're conditioning your mind to accept that there will always be something in your way, and then your mind will see right through whatever that something may be. Not just now, but always. Remember how you got this far and how much of you is already invested.

Here's the really great thing: you only have to go through a fight like this once in your lifetime.

Sure, there'll be other fights, but because of the experience you've gained from this one – the fight of your life – and because you now understand how the Laws of the Universe work, you only have to apply that which you already know to all future bouts.

The real skill, once you weather the storm, is knowing where you want to be. You know where you've come from, so it makes sense that if you're on a journey you know where you're headed.

Often people will weather the storm but have no idea which way to go once the fog clears. This is the time, as Mary Morrissey would say, to 'Dare the Dark and say YES to your dream'.

What she means by this is that even if you can't see what the future holds, if you have a dream you should follow it.

Rags-to-riches guru Gerry Robert, author of *The Millionaire Mindset*, said, 'No matter what, don't hang your dreams in the closet.'

You see, if you hang them in the closet you only see them when you go to the closet. You need to focus on your dreams with passionate desire. Only by doing this will they manifest into reality.

I've learned from personal experience, that almost anything you can imagine you can have in your life. I know this sounds like a throwaway line, but it's not. I continue to prove this to myself on a daily basis. And I watch others do exactly the same.

I met a beautiful lady named Wendy Soderman. At first I was just blown away by her zest for life. After listening to her talk for an hour and a half, I blew my nose, wiped away my tears and walked away thinking how blessed my life has been. Let me give you the short version of Wendy's story, the way I remember it.

Wendy had a terrible upbringing. Her father left when she was young and her mother was involved in all things bad. She had to fend for herself from a very young age and would spend most of her time at school, even after all the other kids had gone home.

The teachers at the school Wendy attended knew that she was special. To help her get away from her miserable life, they changed her grades so that she could go on to college, and hopefully find a better life.

Wendy wanted to teach. Her studying went well, and she met a nice boy whose name was Kris. They were married a few years later, moved to London, Ontario, in Canada and, as planned, Wendy fell pregnant. Soon after, she found out she was having twins.

At 20 weeks into the pregnancy, doctors informed Wendy that one of her identical twins had stopped growing, and that he would probably die in the womb. However, week after week, even though he still hadn't grown, the small twin, Korey, continued to survive. The doctors didn't know why, but still they insisted that he would probably die.

At 32 weeks, the doctors explained that the small twin's heart was failing. They told Wendy that even if he survived, his chances of being born without some kind of mental or physical handicap were not good. They gave Wendy a choice: let the little one die in the womb and hopefully the growing baby, Kyle, would go on for another eight weeks and be born healthy. Or they both had to come out today, within 30 minutes, which would in turn risk the survival of not only Korey, but also Kyle.

The heart-wrenching decision that Wendy and Kris made was to have them both, there and then, to give them both a chance at life.

Kyle was born and weighed 2 kilograms. He almost died in the first few weeks due to the complications of premature delivery. He spent the first month of his life in intensive care before finally going home.

Korey was born and weighed about half a kilogram.

He almost died on a number of occasions and spent his first three months in intensive care.

While Korey lay in hospital fighting for his life, Wendy and Kris would tell their other baby Kyle, who was now at home, how much they loved and adored him. They would then record the same message on a tape recorder and take it to the hospital each day when they visited Korey. They would leave the recorder beside Korey's bed so he could hear the same loving words as his brother, every single day.

Mother's Day was approaching, and as Korey had grown to a massive 1.5 kilograms, the doctors said he could go home. Two days before his pending discharge, Wendy received a call from the hospital telling her that Korey had been rushed into surgery, and that she should hurry to the hospital if she wanted to say goodbye to her son.

On arrival, Wendy and Kris were informed by the doctors that Korey had an intestinal infection, and that because he was so small, and had no chance of survival, they'd sown his little body back up and put him on a respirator. On the clipboard at the end of Korey's bed, one of the doctors or nurses had written 'CRASHED' on his chart. Korey was placed back into a special section of intensive care, with other babies who were expected to die within a day.

Wendy sat with Korey's frail little body, and realised that his desperate fight for life was almost over. She told him she didn't want him to fight any more, and that it was finally time for him to rest.

After many hours at the hospital that day, Wendy kissed her broken baby goodbye and sent him off to heaven.

But Korey didn't die. Instead, he slowly began to recover. The doctors couldn't believe it, nor could they explain it. Unbelievably, three months later, Wendy and Kris took Korey home to see his brother.

At eight months of age, Korey had a CAT scan on his brain. His body wasn't developing and he was only about half the size of his brother, Kyle. The neurologist told Wendy that she should have aborted Korey and never brought him into the world. He said that Korey would be severely growth restricted and that he had cerebral palsy. He also said that Korey would have to be institutionalised and that he would probably never even be able to recognise Wendy, Kris or Kyle.

Every day for the next few years, doctors measured, evaluated and tested every aspect of Korey's physical body and development. They encouraged Wendy to concentrate on their 'good' baby Kyle, and said that Korey would be better in the care of an institution where trained people could look after him.

While friends and family pitied Wendy and Kris, the local media were becoming extremely vocal about their opposition to the choice they made – to risk the life of a healthy baby to save the life of one that would never be healthy or without handicap.

To get away from the pity and blame, and to try and get their lives back on track, Wendy and Kris decided to move their home from Canada to Florida, in the hope that their boys could have a new beginning.

In Florida they found their dream home and were accepted by their new community. That was until Wendy tried to enrol her boys in pre-school. It appeared that when Korey and Kyle turned up for the interview, on every occasion the school had just given out their last spot.

Because she didn't want her boys separated, and after much encouragement from her husband Kris, Wendy decided to open her own school. Using their total savings, she set up a school in a small commercial unit, unlike any other. It was visually appealing, had 3D ships, water features and murals on every wall and door. It was like something out of Disneyland. Wendy would dress up in costume each day while teaching, sometimes as Cinderella, to encourage her students to be creative. All children, including those with special needs, were accepted at Wendy's school. She called it The Ideal School.

At three years of age, Korey was nonverbal, could not walk, sit, stand or feed himself. He could, however, express himself using simple hand gestures in a clumsy manner. He was labelled a quadriplegic since he had no normal functioning limbs.

When he was tested a year or so later, Korey was

found to have an extremely high IQ. The doctors said they'd never seen a child with such intelligence and personality in such a physically challenged body.

After a few years of running the school, Wendy started to receive complaints from headmasters of schools that her students had graduated to. Their complaints were that her students were testing as 'gifted' and that they were well ahead of where other children of the same age were, as far as their IQ was concerned. Of course, this made no sense, and the complaints ended after a while. As the needs of her boys and other children became evident, Wendy expanded her school from just a pre-school to a school that taught from pre-school to Year 5.

At six years of age, Korey was moving around by way of a motorised wheelchair, and communicating by way of hand gestures and a voice computer.

At seven years of age, Korey had surgery to try to stretch his limbs in the hope that one day he would walk, and be able to use his arms.

The surgery and the recovery were extremely painful, and unfortunately had no positive effect on Korey's twisted body. He soon became depressed as he watched his healthy brother enjoying his normal life. Korey went through many dark stages as he got older and was under constant counselling. But the love from Wendy and Kris, and from his twin brother, never came into question. They were a family, and would always be there for Korey . . . no matter what.

Wendy says, 'I remember when the boys were little and they were playing in their room. Korey was lying on the floor – he couldn't sit – and his brother leaned into his face and out of the blue stated: "I'm glad you listened to me in Mummy's tummy and didn't die."'

As the boys grew older, so too did the need to expand The Ideal School to cater for children of older ages. Kris gave up his job and joined Wendy and the team, and they moved the school to bigger and better premises. It was just an old warehouse, but Wendy knew it was right. Just like her first school, this one was designed with the same creative vigour, with murals on the doors and walls, three-dimensional pieces of art and canvases from artists around the globe.

Everything was going well . . . until a hurricane came to Florida. It ripped the roof right off the warehouse and tore the place apart. Everything was ruined. As Wendy and Kris were already at maximum on their credit cards and had a second mortgage on their home, they had no idea how they could possibly afford to rebuild their school.

When news got out that the school had been demolished, tradesmen and builders came knocking on their door with offers of free help. Doctors came, dentists came, architects came, all offering their services or their labour free of charge.

Radio stations got behind the cause, many locals chipped in, and it wasn't too long before the school was rebuilt to its original, and now even better, creative standard.

Finally, after many months, Wendy's school re-opened, to the delight of the local community. Since this time Wendy and Kris have built a new school beside their Ideal School, this one is called the Dream School.

While the Ideal School caters to all children from pre-school to Year 5, the Dream School is for children in Years 6 to 8.

Korey and Kyle are now 18 years old, and while I haven't met Kyle, Korey is a typical teenager, with a heap of attitude and a wonderful sense of humour. I saw him cruising around in his wheelchair one day wearing a T-shirt that read 'I do my own stunts!'.

The reason I wanted to tell this story is to prove to you that when you 'weather the storm', anything is possible. Kris and Wendy Soderman have been through every possible emotion in their lives; they've had their highs and they've certainly had their lows, but the thing that radiates from them is an amazing desire to succeed.

It's hard to explain in words, but their faith in themselves, and their persistence to keep on going no matter what was put before them, is a true testimony as to the love they have for their children, and for each other.

Wendy is about to embark on a public campaign

starting in the United States that will shed some light on why her schools are so successful. If you ever have the chance to see Wendy's presentation, you'll hear about a little red bird that continues to fly in and out of her life. It's a charming story and one I know you'll enjoy.

While I was fortunate enough to meet Wendy, Kris and Korey, you probably know someone just like them. They're just normal, everyday people who have overcome the obstacles put before them and made the decision to win, no matter how many storms they have to weather.

Picture in your mind where you want to be in life, and make the decision, just like Kris and Wendy, to let nothing stop you from getting there.

Every adversity, every failure, every heartache carries with it the seed of an equal or greater benefit.

Napoleon Hill

FIGHTING TIPS

The Gallery of Good and Evil

This is a sure-fire way to remove the obstacles from your life, once and for all.

If you practise this method, pretty soon any person who has a negative effect on you will become so insignificant in your life that you won't even remember why you let them affect you so much. Any obstacle, be it unhealthy food, a competitor's product, a dreary bank balance, an old car that needs updating, an unwanted ex-partner, you name it, will not even rate a mention in your mind or in your life.

Here's how my Gallery of Good and Evil works:

Imagine yourself at a circus carnival and you've just walked up to the shooting gallery. You pick up a rifle and look through the sights and what you see is a line of yellow ducks rolling along the belt.

Now, here's the fun part. In your mind, I want you to replace those ducks with round metal plates, about as big as a softball. I want you to think of all the people in your life, your friends, your family, your pets, your neighbours, your ex-partners, your workmates, your boss, etc., and transpose their faces onto the round plates rolling along the belt.

What you now see are the faces of the people in your life. Most of them will be smiling at you. These are the 'good ones'. The ones who aren't smiling are the ones that affect your life in a negative way. Let's call them the 'bad ones'.

I want you to pick up your rifle and aim it at the faces rolling along the belt. This is a laser rifle, so as you line up the faces on the belt you'll see a red dot appear on them if your aim is true.

As the faces roll around, whenever you see a face that isn't smiling, shoot it down (metaphorically speaking, of course). Now stop for a second. That face is now down. Watch the belt, and as the faces continue to pass, you'll notice that the one you shot down is still down. Every time it rolls past it is still down.

Okay, get back on the sights of the rifle and find the next unsmiling face. When it comes around, shoot it down. You'll now notice that both of these faces stay down every time they pass.

Now the next one. And the next. Continue to shoot down the unsmiling faces rolling along the belt. When you're finished, the only faces you'll see will be smiling faces.

Put the laser rifle down and continue to watch the gallery of faces roll by you on the conveyor belt. Memorise this picture in your mind. Every time you go back to your 'people gallery', you'll only see the smiling faces, the good ones; the people who affect your life in a positive way.

You'll never see the bad ones, because you've already removed them from the gallery in your own mind, and now that you can't see them, you won't think about them or focus on them or their opinions ever again.

Okay, so now you've removed the 'bad people' from your life. It's now time to remove the other obstacles using the same gallery method.

This time on the round plates, imagine all the things you want in your life: your dream home, your new car, your perfect partner, a pile of money, a plate of fruit, a new wardrobe, a beautiful holiday; as well as all of the things you don't want in your life: like a big pile of bills, fatty food, ill health, out-of-date furniture, an unhealthy bank balance, too much work, or whatever it is.

As these items roll along the belt, take aim and shoot down the things you don't want in your life. It's easy, just shoot 'em down.

What you're now looking at is a gallery of all the things you want to have in your life. Memorise this picture in your mind. Every time you go back to your 'obstacle gallery' you'll only see the things that you truly want.

Be sure to go back to your galleries on a daily basis. The great thing about these galleries is that you can add and remove obstacles and people as desired. Each day when you go into your galleries, you're reaffirming what you want, and forgetting about what you don't.

And the more you focus on what you want, the sooner the Universe will bring it into alignment.

Remember, prosperity is a mindset. And because it's a mindset it can mean a lot of different things to a lot of different people. If you can hold it in your head, you can hold it in your hand.

ROUND 7

SECOND WIND

It's all downhill from here. Six rounds down and only four to go. In this round I'll get my second wind. BREATHE DEEP. What this means is that I've totally exhausted all of my strength and fitness in the first six rounds, and, thanks to my dedicated training, I now get a renewed burst of energy, so much so that I feel I can do it all over again. This is a good round to take control of the fight once and for all, and concentrate on winning. JAB, JAB. It's also a good opportunity to show gratitude for my skills and stamina, and for all the reasons and the people who got me this far.

You've got to be feeling good at this stage. The path forward is clear. You've overcome the obstacles again and again. You've looked inside yourself and what you found was courage and determination. You know you're headed for greatness and you can clearly picture your future life.

Now is a good time to go over what you've learned from this fight so it's clearly locked inside you for future journeys.

When Muhammad Ali defeated George Foreman he got his second wind in Round 8. He'd been through the same process that you've just been through, and as he set his sights on winning, he took stock of everything he'd learned in his life to that point, before making his claim to the title of 'the best fighter the world has ever seen'.

Reflect on the lessons you've learned in this fight so far. These lessons are priceless and can't be purchased for any amount of money.

Sit back now and take a deep breath. Just like Dr Martin Luther King, you're at the top of the mountain and you can see the Promised Land.

You need to keep your mind open to all possibilities, as you are now vibrating at a much higher level than you previously were. This is a good time to show gratitude to the Universe.

'Uh-oh, you've lost me,' I hear you say. Let me explain. By showing gratitude, or being grateful for the wonderful things already in your life, you continue to vibrate on a higher level. When you do this you feel better about yourself, and when you feel better about yourself you attract better things into your life.

Remember, when you're feeling down and bad about yourself you attract more of the same, because you're vibrating at a lower level.

When you lift your vibration level, you only attract that which is vibrating at the same level. So the higher you vibrate, the better you feel about yourself, and the better things you attract into your life.

The Universal Law of Attraction is based on this. It simply finds vibrations on the same level and puts them together. The thing to remember here is that your vibrations don't come from what you say; they come from what you're thinking and how you're feeling. Just because you tell people you're feeling great doesn't mean you'll be attracting great things. You can't fool the Universe. It doesn't even hear words; it just feels vibrations and sends matching vibrations together.

Dr Michael Beckwith told me that the best way to ensure that my vibrations start at the right level is to think of the things I'm grateful for every morning before I get out of bed. I do that every day now. I thank the Universe for my life, for my beautiful family, for the beautiful views from my apartment, for my friends, and also for the opportunities of the new day.

This is a great way to start every day, and it ensures that you're vibrating on a high level before you even get out of bed.

The Law of Increase says, 'What you praise and show gratitude to, you will have more of in your life.'

Up until a few years ago, I had no idea how I'd achieved what I had in my life. But then I learned about the Law of Attraction and instantly the penny dropped.

In 1990 my staff bought me a framed picture of a Porsche 911. I'd just bought a new Toyota Celica and there was no way I could afford a Porsche, but I put the picture on my office wall. Every single day from then on, I imagined myself sitting in the Porsche. I imagined how the seats would feel and how the leather would smell and how the engine would sound. I had no idea how I could ever afford a Porsche, but I knew one day I would have one.

Three years later I bought my first Porsche. It

wasn't a 911 like the one in the picture, but it was still a Porsche.

Just two years after that I bought my first Porsche 911, just like the one in the picture on my office wall. Words can't really explain how good it felt to be driving in a car that, up until now, I'd only ever dreamed about.

What I can tell you, though, is that it made me feel so confident when I drove it.

At this stage I was single and dating regularly. I'd jump in my Porsche, pick up my date for the evening and drive to the city. Although it was a good hour's drive either way, I loved the drive almost as much as I loved dining at any of the wonderful restaurants at Darling Harbour, one of Sydney's famous attractions.

At Darling Harbour I would sit with my date for the evening and stare at the city skyline, one of the most beautiful sights in the world. I'd imagine myself waking up in the morning and seeing these views from where I lived, or sitting on my balcony at night with a glass of red, marvelling at the beauty of the neon city.

I had no idea how I would do this, as the house I then owned was valued at $145,000 with a mortgage of $135,000 secured against it. And I knew that any apartment with the type of views I wanted would be valued at over $1 million. But I was passionate and I never let the picture in my mind fade.

I knew I would do it. I didn't know how, but I knew I would.

Five years went by and I found myself living in the city. Not just in an apartment with city views, but possibly the best apartment with the most spectacular views of the city and the Harbour Bridge that Sydney has to offer.

A few years ago, if you'd asked me how I did it I wouldn't have been able to tell you. Yet today I know exactly how I did it. I had a passionate desire to succeed and I focused on winning. Never once did I change my mind and say, 'It's all too hard, I think I'll settle for something less.' I visualised in my mind what I wanted, and the Law of Attraction had no option but to bring it to me.

Every night now, when I lay my head on my pillow, the last thing I see before I close my eyes to sleep is the amazing Harbour Bridge. I feel so blessed, and I thank the Universe constantly.

When your second wind comes, use it wisely. Take the time to go over what you've learned and remember to show gratitude for the beautiful things and people you already have in your life.

Hope lies in the dreams of one's imagination and in the courage of those who dare to make dreams into reality.

Jonas Salk

FIGHTING TIPS

Hang up the phone

When I'm trying to be in 'that place' I want to be in, you know, the place that makes me feel my best, I really don't want too many distractions. When you find yourself in 'that place', you almost need to go back in time about 100 years and ignore anything that runs on power. Let me explain . . .

You start to feel good about yourself because you can see in your mind just how great your future is looking. But then you turn on the TV and you see the news of the world, telling you about mayhem and death and tragedy. Or you turn on the radio and all you hear are people complaining about their lives, or about how crooked some politician is. Or you turn on your computer and browse the net and every home page has the same story about plane crashes and cyclones and that Paris Hilton has been released from jail. Again. Or you answer the phone and it's someone telling you how silly you are for believing in what you do and that you really should come back to reality.

All you need to do is HANG UP THE PHONE. When you're in 'that place', my advice to you is this: don't watch television, don't listen to talk-back radio, don't read the newspapers, don't browse the net, and don't take phone calls from too-caring friends.

Remove yourself from everyday life, just for a while, and you'll be amazed at how much better your time at 'that place' will be.

In the last 12 months I've rarely watched the news on TV. When I'm driving I mainly listen to CDs of music and people that I like. I can't remember the last time I bought a news-paper. And I just don't listen to or associate with negative people who drain my energy. Yet I feel no less educated and no less knowledgeable than I did when all of these things were a part of my daily routine. I now get just enough information to have an understanding of what's going on . . . and never more. I don't need more.

When I'm watching television I even find myself switch-ing channels when a real-life sad or depressing medical story comes on, or when a crime show depicts how a mass-murderer carved up and hid 27 bodies. They're just too depressing and they move my vibration down to a very low level, which in turn attracts only those things also vibrating at the same low level.

And yet I still love watching a great horror flick at the movies. Go figure!

Here's the thing, you need to know what's happening around you even though a lot of it is sad or depressing. So what I do is I take in the headlines, and then move on. Whether it's TV, radio, newspapers or word of mouth, I just take in enough information to keep me informed, and then I go back to the things that make me happy and uplift me, like my favourite music, TV shows that make me laugh, or my favourite books.

If you do this, your vibration will only be 'down' for a short period, and you'll always be heading back to an 'up' vibration. Of course the higher your vibration, the better things you'll attract into your life.

When it comes to bad things in our world, we need to be informed, BUT WE DON'T NEED TO BE INUNDATED.

Remember this tip, it will serve you well as you move on to your new life of bigger, better and brighter things.

ROUND 8

DECIDE TO WIN

What a terrific round this one is. I can almost smell victory from here. RIGHT CROSS. My ribs are sore and my legs are tired but I have my second wind and I'm thinking with a clear mind. Now is the time to make a decision. Only three rounds to go. LEFT HOOK. The hard work is behind me. I have the desire. I have the faith in myself. Just one thing left to do . . . Decide to Win!

In life, this is sometimes the hardest thing to do. It makes no difference how much training you've done, how much pain you've been through, how much you've learned, how much you've read, or how much you've listened, if you're not prepared to make a decision to take action.

I know people who go to seminars weekly yet never seem to improve their lifestyle. Sure, they are nice people, and yes, they are highly motivated. But the problem is that they are only motivated enough to go to the next seminar.

When you make the decision to take action, you're making the decision to win. You see, by taking action you've actually made the decision to go after what you want. And, as Napoleon Hill says, 'Desire backed by faith knows no such word as impossible.'

Doug Wead taught me that when I make a decision, a great power is unleashed. Millions of people

THE FIGHTER WITHIN

around the world know this to be true.

I've personally found that when I make the decision to take action, it feels as if a heavy burden has been removed from my life. It's a good feeling because you're giving in to what you know is right. Every cell in your entire body relaxes, knowing that they're all now working for the same cause.

The sooner you make the decision to take action, the sooner your life will start to show you the results you desire. It doesn't matter where you are in life when you make the decision. What matters is you know where you're headed.

Some people might say, 'But you already have money, it's easier for you', or, 'Well, when I have enough money behind me, then I'll decide.' But it doesn't work like that. The problem is that until you make the decision to take action you will never have enough money behind you.

This is a tough decision that very few people actually make. Donald Trump made it. Warren Buffet made it. Bill Gates made it. At one stage in their lives, before they were wealthy, three of the richest people in the world made the decision to take action.

Muhammad Ali made it the day he accepted the fight with George Foreman. Danny from the motorbike accident made it as he lay in hospital.

Until you make the decision to win, your goose will be laying hard-boiled eggs, and the pot at the end of your rainbow will only be full of dirt.

106

When you have the knowledge that you now have, it's almost an injustice not to decide to go forward. It's like being a fighter who trains seven days a week for a year but never steps in the ring.

Bob Proctor, who I believe is one of the best motivational speakers on the planet, and who probably has a better understanding of the Laws of the Universe than any person I've ever met, says: 'People who won't make a decision to be successful are planning their own failure. They don't know that they're planning it, but they are.

'If people are not creating their own future, then it is being created for them, by default.

'Every person alive is at the centre of their Universe. Just as you are the centre of yours, I am the centre of mine. Not only am I at the centre of my own universe, but I'm also the star of it.

'People who won't decide to succeed see themselves as extras in their own movie.'

If you don't dare to dream about how beautiful your future can be, you are robbing yourself, and those around you, of a life full of plenty and abundance.

We all have a 'right' to dream, but we have a 'duty' to succeed. When asked the question, almost 100 per cent of people will choose rich over poor. Why then do only around 5 per cent actually go after being rich?

The answer is simple: fear. The 95 per cent of people who choose poor over rich are afraid of leaving their comfort zone. They're afraid of what they will have to give up to have a life of wealth and plenitude. They're afraid of leaving their family and friends behind.

You see, being wealthy is a mindset. A lot of people don't think they deserve to be wealthy. Well, I'm here to tell you that everyone deserves to have a lifetime of abundance, and to have love and riches beyond their wildest dreams.

To achieve this life of plenty, you need to clearly see the picture in your mind of your life at its most perfect. You then need to surround that picture with emotion and desire. And finally, you need to make a conscious decision that this is what you will settle for and nothing less.

If you do this, I guarantee that your life will improve continually, and the more you want that perfect life, and the longer you can hold that picture in your mind, the better your life will become.

Everyone deserves to be wealthy, but only a few will make the decision to win.

It doesn't matter where you think you are in life right now. I'd rather be a poor battler who can hold a vision in his mind than a multi-millionaire who can't. The poor battler's journey has just begun and can only be limited by his thinking, while the multi-millionaire has gone as far as he will go.

You owe it to yourself to decide to win. And when you do this you will notice that yours isn't the only life that will reap the benefits. Those close to you and those around you will also be affected by your decision. This is what I call the vacuum effect.

When you start to head in an upward direction, the people around you grab on to your feet as you go. They too are now headed in an upward direction. The people around them grab on to their feet and are also pulled up in the vacuum.

Picture this: there's you at the top heading upwards. There are two people on your feet. There are four people on the feet of those on your feet. And so on, and so on.

The vacuum effect is sucking those around you up in your success. How cool is that, knowing that where you're headed you'll have some friends and loved ones with you?

So much for the fear of leaving your family and friends behind. You see, that fear, or rather that excuse, is just an obstacle. And obstacles become invisible when you focus on the reward.

Let's look at some other obstacles that will stop you from making a decision to succeed.

'Afraid of leaving your comfort zone.' A comfort zone to me is not somewhere I'm trying to leave. Yet by reading this book, you're obviously trying to work out how to get out of your comfort zone. How comfortable can it be if you are trying to escape it?

'What do I have to give up?' What do you actually have right now that you wouldn't be prepared to give up in exchange for a life of plenitude and abundance?

There isn't a thing I own that I wouldn't trade for this reward.

You see, when you decide to win, there is no limit to what you can have. If it's money you choose, you can have as much as you want. If it is love you're after, you can have the most fulfilling relationships. If it is business success, or weight loss, or better health, you can have it if you'll only make the decision to win.

Remember, we are not limited by money, but by the poverty of our dreams.

When you decide to win, and I know I've said those words a lot in this round, the rest of your life will fall into place. When a fighter makes that decision to win in the eighth round, he has no chance of losing the fight. The next two rounds are just a formality as he goes about planning how to celebrate his win.

Think about that now. How will you celebrate your win?

Our life is defined by the quality of the questions we're prepared to ask.

Mary Morrissey

FIGHTING TIPS

The Elevator Theory

For those of you who think you're too far down the chain, or that you don't have enough money to make a decision to succeed right now, let me explain it like this:

Imagine your goal, your dream, your pot of gold, is located on the top floor of a 50-storey building.

And imagine that you get into the elevator at the basement. You push the button to the fiftieth floor and the doors close.

Guess what? You've made the decision and you're now on your way. Now that wasn't too hard, was it? You see, the decision you need to make is only in your mind. And when you make the decision to take action in your mind, as Dr Michael Beckwith says, 'The Universe will correspond to the nature of your song.'

Okay, so the elevator is on its way to the fiftieth floor. Suddenly it stops at level 3 and somebody gets in. This person is also on the way to the fiftieth floor.

Then it stops at level 6 and somebody else gets in. Then at levels 9, 14, 23, 29, 36, and so on. And guess what? All of these people are going to the same floor, level 50.

Finally the elevator stops at level 50. The doors open and, believe it or not, everyone in the elevator gets out and heads in the direction of their reward.

Here's the question: Do you think it now matters on which level of the building you entered the elevator?

Of course it doesn't, and what this proves is that it doesn't matter where you are in life right now when you make the decision to win. Whether you're in the basement or on the forty-ninth level, it makes no difference to the Universe. Remember, the Law of Attraction simply finds vibrations on the same level and puts them together.

Now let's look at the Elevator Theory again, but this time just a little differently. You've now been to the fiftieth level and you know what's there. It's now five years later: you have a new dream, a new direction, and a new challenge in your life.

This next scenario will help you to understand just how much you really want what you're going after. If you answer 'yes' to the last question, then you should absolutely continue heading in that direction. If you answer 'no', maybe you should check to see if you're really going after what you want.

You're on the basement level again. You push the button

to summon the elevator, but it doesn't come. It's out of order. Do you take the stairs or do you wait?

If you take the stairs you know you'll be totally exhausted by the time you reach level 50, if you even reach it at all. But you already know that on level 50 there's an abundance of everything. You've been there and you've seen it with your own eyes.

If you wait it may take days for the elevator to be repaired. Maybe you won't be as motivated in a few days? Maybe you'll be more motivated?

Last time when you made the decision it was easy. This time it's going to be difficult.

The question to ask yourself is this: Do I take the stairs?

FIGHT LIKE YOU'VE ALREADY WON

Although my body is bruised and battered, my mind is fresh and invigorated in Round 9. Only two rounds to go and I know that all I have to do is stay on my feet – JAB AND MOVE – and not get tagged with any big shots. Not only can I see the referee raising my arm in victory, I can now feel the referee's hand on my arm. STRAIGHT RIGHT. It's now so very real, and so very close. Because in my mind I've already won, I can now fight like the champion I am. My posture becomes straighter, my punches become crisper, and I'm moving around the ring like it's Round 1 again. I'm full of confidence and overflowing with desire.

DOUBLE JAB. The faith I have in my own ability is limitless. I'm fighting like I've already won.

I can't think of a better way to start this round than to share with you something that Dr Michael Beckwith said to me: 'Put yourself in the future – see yourself – then look back to the present, and find out how you got there.'

Dr Beckwith really is one of the world's great spiritual teachers, and he believes that the three tenses of time – the past, the present, and the future – have already happened. Just as we can look to the past for answers, we can also look to the future. When we visualise where we want to be in our future lives, what we see is what has already happened. The key now is working out how to get there.

As I embark on my own spiritual journey, I find affirmation in the Universal Laws and see that Dr Beckwith's theory is easy to accept.

Think about your own life for a moment. Can you remember picturing yourself in that new dress, or driving that new car, or in your new home, or on that beautiful holiday, and then, when you're actually in that dress or that car or that home, or you're on that holiday, you think to yourself that this is exactly how you pictured it?

If any of the pictures you've held in your mind have ever come to fruition, then you won't have too much trouble accepting this theory either.

What if he's right? Think about that for a moment. What if he really is right; and the future has already happened? What are we missing out on in our lives?

If our thoughts create our future and we're always thinking 'not enough' and 'lack of', then we're creating a future of 'not enough' and 'lack of'. Make sense?

But if our thoughts are of 'beauty' and of 'plenty' and of 'abundance' then we're creating a future based around those thoughts.

Imagine if, instead of only 5 per cent of people thinking in this positive way, what would happen if 50 per cent or 75 per cent of people started thinking in the same positive way? Would we be creating a totally different world in the future to the one that most people are now picturing . . . one of drought, and hunger, and war, and poverty?

I have to believe that the answer here is YES. It's hard to believe, but it's even harder not to believe.

Round 9 is the round when you stand tall. You've pictured success and overcome every obstacle in your path. Now you need to live like you already have it.

For example, if your 'winning' was to live in a new home, it's time now to feel like you're already living there. If it was to own a new car, feel like you already have it.

I call it 'finding that place' (see the Fighting Tips at the end of Round 2) as it's the place to go to when you need to feel good.

If you can imagine yourself in your new home, pottering in the garden, bathing by the pool, relaxing with your family in your state of-the-art entertainment room, the feeling you'll get will lift your vibration to its highest level. And when this happens, you will attract into your life only those things vibrating at the same high level.

Bob Proctor has a great way of testing out this theory. He once asked me at a seminar: 'What did you do tomorrow?'

Of course I had no idea what he was talking about, so I asked, 'What do you mean, Bob?'

In exactly the same tone, he said, 'Tell me what you did tomorrow.'

I thought about this for a moment, but before I could reply Bob stated, 'I think you need to have your memory replaced, because it's not a good memory that only works in one direction.'

Okay, so it took a while, but I finally got it. What Bob was actually asking me was what did I do in my mind tomorrow? This drove home the point that if I wasn't creating in my mind what I wanted and where

I wanted to be tomorrow, it would be created for me by default.

As human beings we have the power to create our future by way of what we focus on. By focusing on our dreams, our goals, our visions, and by feeling like we already have them, we are co-creating with the Universe that which we want in our lives.

And the Law of Attraction says 'and so you shall have it'.

When I need to feel good, I 'find that place' in my PAST that made me feel great and I go there in my mind.

When I need to feel good, I 'find that place' in my FUTURE that makes me feel great and I go there in my mind.

The memory really does work in both directions. Bob was right.

You see, whether I'm remembering the beautiful times in my past, or thinking about my successes to come in the future, I'm vibrating at that high level. If my future doesn't look so temporarily bright I can go back to my past to make me feel good. If my past doesn't look so bright I can go to my future to feel good. Whether I need to look to the past or to the future, there is a place I can find to get me feeling better. And once I'm feeling good, I'm attracting good.

Let me break this down to its simplest form – if you think you're a loser, you'll be correct. And if you think you're a winner, you'll also be correct.

Henry Ford once said, 'Whether you think you can or you can't, either way you'll be right.'

This means that if you persistently focus with desire and faith on being rich; and you can actually see yourself as rich, you will be rich. If you persistently focus with desire and faith on being at your perfect weight, and you can actually see yourself at your perfect weight, you will achieve it. The easiest way to achieve what you want is to vibrate on the same level. Simply put, live your life now like you've already achieved your goal.

Think and feel like you're already rich. Go and see your new home, walk through it, and get the feeling of what it will be like to live there. Go test-drive that new Mercedes. Put the top down and experience that feeling. If you're trying to lose weight, go shopping now for the new clothes you'll soon be wearing. Feel the material, hold them against your body, and buy them if you have to. Whatever you need to do to get that feeling started, do it. Because once you get into the vibration of where you want to be, or what you want in your life, you will start to attract these things to you.

It's important that you do this. I guarantee that your current life will improve immediately and constantly once you master this trait.

Remember this: as you move towards success, success moves towards you. Don't hold negative or sad thoughts and images in your mind for too long. The Law of Attraction works on these vibrations exactly the same way as it does on the positive and happy ones. And you don't want more of the same negative or sad things coming into your life, do you?

When I was 13 years old, there was a kid in my football team called Sam, who, after a short illness, ended up in hospital. The doctors couldn't work out what was making Sam ill, so they decided to do a whole load of tests on him and take dozens of x-rays to try to find out. The next time I saw his parents, they told me that Sam was still in the hospital and he was having some serious treatment. They said he had throat cancer.

Now, at 13 years of age, you don't really know much about cancer, only what you hear from your parents, and that was that Sam was going to die. I remember me and some other kids from the team would go to the hospital to see Sam, and when we'd arrive, his parents, who were always there, told us not to talk about the cancer in front of Sam, because it made him too upset.

So, we'd sit in the hospital with our friend, who had a tube coming out of his throat, and think how lucky we were that we didn't have the cancer. Funny thing was that Sam would always be so upbeat, always laughing and making jokes about how he looked and how he couldn't wait to get out of there.

We would leave his room, me and the other kids,

and we would cry all the way home knowing that our friend was dying.

Every weekend we'd get on a bus and go and see Sam in hospital, and every week he'd be looking thinner and thinner, and sicker and sicker. Still, every week he'd make us laugh with his jokes and his quick wit. We all tried to be brave and play along, and we'd laugh out loud, but every now and then one of us would break down and cry.

Sam would say, 'What are you crying for, dummy, I'll be out of here soon, you watch.'

After a month or two some of the kids stopped going to the hospital on the weekend, it was just too traumatic for them. But for those of us who continued to go, his parents would always say, 'Remember not to talk about the cancer.' And we never did.

The last time we visited Sam in hospital, on the way out his parents pulled the four of us 13-year-olds aside and suggested that we didn't come back to visit for a while as it was taking too much out of him. And we never did.

We left the hospital that day and never spoke about Sam at all. In fact, on the way home on the bus, we never said a word to each other. I knew we were all thinking the same thing . . . that we'd never see our friend again.

Sam spent almost five months in hospital and had massive doses of chemotherapy and radiation treatment. Then, one afternoon at football training, a car drove up close to the field where we were playing. It was Sam's parents' car. It had been almost four weeks since we'd last been to the hospital and I braced myself for the news I was about to hear. I felt my stomach churn and my eyes well up with tears. As the other kids noticed the car, they just stopped where they were. Some sat down, preparing for the news.

But the strangest thing happened. The car door opened and out jumped Sam. He had a bandage around his throat and he looked pretty skinny, and he didn't have much hair, but it was definitely Sam.

Nobody moved. I don't think anybody believed what they were seeing. Sam walked over and shook my hand, which was kind of strange because up until then we'd never shaken hands before. We were only 13. The other kids slowly made their way over to where we were standing.

After more handshakes, Sam told us how good it was to be out of hospital and to be eating decent food again. He said he probably wouldn't be able to play again this season, but that he'd be back and ready for next year.

We all talked for a while, then Sam walked back to his dad's car and they drove off. To every 13-year-old kid that day, we thought we'd just witnessed a miracle.

True to his word, Sam did come back to play football the following season. Strangely enough, nobody ever spoke about his illness.

It wasn't until a few years later that one day, after

a game, I asked Sam how he beat his cancer. What he told me made no sense to my 15-year-old brain, and only started to make sense dozens of years later.

Sam told me that he never knew he had cancer. He said his parents never told him. All they said was that he was sick and that he would get a lot sicker before he got better. And that's exactly what happened.

When I think back about Sam and his cancer, I now understand how he beat it. You see, his mind was never limited by the word 'cancer'. To a lot of people, due to their conditioning, this word means death, or, at best, lots of pain and suffering.

Sam never heard the word, so his mind didn't close down and think the worst. Everyone else who heard the word 'cancer' thought Sam would die. But he didn't hear it. All he heard was that he would get worse before he got better.

Sam's mind never thought of fear or panic, so he was never vibrating on a low level. His thoughts were always that he would get better, and he couldn't wait till that day. Of course this kept his vibration high, and when your vibration is high and you're feeling good, you attract only that which vibrates at the same level.

The lesson here is that Sam fought like he had already won. Thanks to his parents, he never saw the obstacles between himself and good health. He just saw the end reward, and that was him getting better.

From Sam's experience I now know that the sooner we can get into that place where we feel like we already have what we want in our lives, the sooner these things will come. Make no mistake, the Universe is never wrong. If you need proof, just look at nature. Grass grows, rivers run, despite what man does to stop them. Seasons follow each other with no encouragement or explanation whatsoever. Every day is followed by night. The Laws that govern the Universe are not open to negotiation.

What we receive in our lives is what we attract to our lives, never more, never less. Look to the future, see yourself with the things that you want in your life, and live your life NOW like you already have them.

Just like I have, you too can follow Sam's lead, and fight like you've already won.

If you really want to do something, you'll find a way. If you don't, you'll find an excuse.

Jim Rohn

FIGHTING TIPS

Make a Vision Board

If you're serious about having the things in your life that you want, you really need to have one of these.

A Vision Board is a board on which you pin pictures of the things you really want. For example, if you want a new car, find a picture of that car and pin it on your Vision Board.

If it's a new home you're after, do the same, find a picture of the home you want and pin it on your board.

If you're dieting, find a picture of a person who has the body that you're after and pin it on your board.

You can do it with anything. If you're after money, write out a cheque from the Bank of the Universe with the exact amount of money you're after, and pin it on your board.

Now place your Vision Board on your desk or near your

computer at work, or somewhere that you'll see it dozens of times a day. Every time you look at the board, imagine that you already have the things on it. Picture yourself driving your new car, or wearing that new diamond ring, or living in that beautiful home. Get that feeling of what it would be like to already have these things.

Your Vision Board doesn't have to be limited to material things only. Find a picture of a couple in a park and visualise yourself walking hand in hand on a bright, sunny day with the one you love. Cut out a picture of a backpack and imagine yourself on a backpacking holiday with your family. Or pin a picture on your Board of an Olympic track and field champion and every time you look at it, imagine yourself running in that local marathon you always said you would.

Once you've looked at your Vision Board a couple of times, your mind will realise how good it makes you feel, and it will lock that feeling into memory. No matter how bad you're feeling, every time you look at your Vision Board your mind will let loose that beautiful endorphin that will have you feeling wonderful again.

And guess what? When you're feeling wonderful you start to attract wonderful things. So the more you look at your Vision Board, the more wonderful you'll feel. And the more wonderful things you'll attract into your life.

Make yourself a Vision Board, update it continually as your wants change, and believe that what you can see, you can have in your life.

Remember, 'Whatever the mind can conceive and believe, the mind can achieve.'

CELEBRATE YOUR SUCCESS

This is the best round of the fight. I know that in just three minutes time I'll be crowned the victor. LEFT RIP, RIGHT RIP. If you look closely you'll see I'm actually smiling as I dance around the ring. I can't even be hit, let alone beaten. I'm thinking about the congratulatory kiss from my partner. DOUBLE JAB. I'm imagining spending my fight purse on an overseas holiday. I feel great and I'm already celebrating my win. My persistence, faith and desire throughout the fight have put me in this frame of mind. BOB AND WEAVE. Even though I don't know it right now, I am unbeatable, for while I'm vibrating on such a high level, only good can be attracted. And although the fight isn't yet over, ladies and gentlemen, we have a winner!

Think about that for a second. The fight's not over but I'm already celebrating my victory.

To most people this concept is hard to accept. Some would say I'm too cocky. Others would be hoping I get knocked out in the final round, because I'm far too confident and far too happy.

To these people my book will be of even greater value. You see, when you celebrate the success of others in a genuine way, you actually start to feel good inside, which in turn lifts your own vibration and attracts better things to your life.

When you're unhappy about the success of others, even those you've never met, you feel angry inside, which lowers your vibration, attracting only the same.

When you enjoy the success of others, you are actually attracted to that success by default.

Let me share with you just a few examples of stories I've heard over the years.

A young child watches a basketball grand final and, as he idolises the Most Valued Player, he says to himself: 'One day I want to be just like him.' Sure enough, 15 years later that young child plays in the same basketball grand final that his idol played in all those years before, and he turns out to be one of the best players in the team. And it all started from celebrating the success of somebody else.

There's the young girl watching television after school who sees the story of a successful woman making some great achievements in the business world and says to herself: 'I want to be successful just like her when I grow up.' Twelve years later, she owns and runs her own business that turns over more than $2 million a year, and sits on the board of three other companies.

Then there's the overweight father who wishes he had more energy to play with his children outdoors. He sees an advertisement for someone who recently lost 35 kilos through diet and exercise, and says to himself: 'I can do that.' Twelve months later he accepts an award for losing more weight than anyone in his program, but more importantly, he is now able to spend more time playing outdoors with his children.

Successful people influence others even if they don't know they're doing it. So celebrate the success of others even if it only makes you FEEL good. Once you can truly celebrate the success of others, it becomes easier to celebrate your own success.

CELEBRATE YOUR SUCCESS

It's important to celebrate YOUR success as soon as you possibly can. When you've pictured in your mind what you want or where you want to be, and you've backed that vision with faith and desire and persistence, it's only a matter of time before you will achieve what you want.

The sooner you start to FEEL like you already have it, and start to celebrate your success, the sooner it will manifest into your life. The Universal Law of Attraction says so. You need to start planning what you'll do when you have that perfect body, or you find that perfect partner, or you have all of that money. And don't plan small, plan big.

Remember, remove the limits (the obstacles) you've placed in your own mind and believe you can have anything you want. Donald Trump says, 'You have to think, so you may as well think big.'

Co-author of *Chicken Soup for the Soul*, and one of the world's most highly sought-after motivational speakers, Mark Victor Hansen has sold more than 144 million books. Mark teaches people to aim as high as they possibly can. When asked how much one should aim for, Mark replied, 'Become as wealthy as you possibly can, because it allows you to say NO.'

He believes that if you make $1 million you can have a great life. But if you make $100 million you can have a great life experience. You see, Mark believes that if we make billions, we can give millions away.

He says that when you have everything you could possibly want, you can then go and find a 'cause'. His 'cause' is to eradicate illiteracy worldwide. He tells the story of when he was a child and being out with his father who couldn't read or write. Mark needed to use the bathroom and his father was so embarrassed when he had to ask someone which was the correct bathroom to take his son to.

From this day on, even as a child, Mark knew that one day he would do something to ensure that nobody else would feel the way his father had, because they couldn't read or write.

He has certainly built much emotion into this 'cause' over the years, and he's now at a stage in his life where he can do something about it. Of course you need some heavy money to wipe out illiteracy. And you also need some creative ideas. It's a massive task for anyone to attempt, but if anyone can do it, Mark Victor Hansen is that person.

When you remove the limits and boundaries of your current thinking and let your mind imagine success with no boundaries, you start to create more than wealth solutions for yourself. You start to think, 'Well, if I have this much, I can look after so many more people.' Then it becomes causes. Soon you'll be looking for solutions to global hunger, even illiteracy, like Mark Victor Hansen.

Let me give you an example. I was recently in the beautiful city of San Diego, sitting in an outdoor café having breakfast. After only being in San Diego for 24 hours, I'd already noticed that there were a lot of homeless people walking around, but one in particular changed my thinking forever.

A young boy aged about 16 started digging through the garbage bin just outside the café. He pulled out a piece of uneaten pancake and a crust that had been thrown away. While he stood there feasting on someone's leftovers, I could tell he hadn't washed in weeks, as his skin was covered in dirt and grease and his hair was knotted and filthy. His clothes were torn and shredded.

As I watched him walk away I started to feel sad and depressed, not the way I normally like to feel. I'd just finished my poached eggs but hadn't touched my toast, and because it was late in coming from the kitchen, the waitress had brought me a complimentary fresh cup of coffee. I grabbed some jam and butter from the table next to mine, picked up the plate with my untouched toast and the fresh coffee, and chased after the young homeless kid.

I caught up with him just before he was about to board an escalator leading up to a small shopping plaza. I handed him the plate with toast and jam and said, 'For you.'

He hesitated for a moment then looked at me humbly, and touching his chest he asked, 'For me?'

I smiled and said, 'For you.' He took the plate as if it were a Christmas dinner, and in a tiny voice said, 'Thank you, sir.'

I then extended the coffee towards him, to which he again asked, 'For me?'

I nodded yes.

Again, in his little mousey voice, he said, 'Thank you, sir.'

I then reached into my pocket and pulled out a five-dollar note and offered it to him. After seeing this boy's face light up like he'd just received his first bike, I wasn't sure who would start crying first, me or him. I quickly handed it over, received his timid but sincere offer of gratitude, patted him on the shoulder and turned and walked away.

As I headed back to the café I could feel the tears rolling down my cheeks and I knew I'd just come to a crossroad in my life. I sat for a moment and started to think. For some strange reason, at that moment, I felt invigorated and full of life and thought. I actually started to feel good and I could feel my vibration lifting.

I thought to myself: if helping just one person makes me feel so good, imagine how I would feel if I was helping hundreds or thousands of people in the same way?

I've found my calling. My reason for being here. You see, my life is already beautiful and extremely fulfilling. Of course there are still things I want to do, but I already feel blessed.

I didn't realise it until then, but there was a cause I'd been looking for and now I'd found it. How I would do this thing I had no idea. But I knew that if I could hold the results I was looking for in my mind, the Universe and its Laws would take care of the rest.

One thing I do know is that I will need many, many millions of dollars to have even the slightest impact on the world's homeless. However, everything is created twice, first in the mind . . . so I guess I'm halfway there.

While my gesture to the young San Diego boy made me feel good, I quickly realised that it would have little or no effect on him. Tomorrow he would still be homeless. He may now believe that there are some kind humans out there, but he'll still be homeless.

The point here is this: become as wealthy as you possibly can and never feel guilty for doing so. Create as much money, and as many beautiful possessions, and as much love and happiness in your life as you could ever want. Travel the world and enjoy your life . . . you deserve it.

However, when you get to that stage when you have everything you want, remember to find YOUR 'cause'. Search for it, prioritise it, emotionalise it, and be sure to persist with it, until you're absolutely satisfied with its result. You don't have to be a politician or a celebrity to improve the world you live in.

Imagine, if you will, your perfect life. A life that sees you in the arms of your perfect partner. A life that sees you with more money than you could ever need. A life that sees you at your perfect weight and shape. A life that sees you in perfect health. A life of unbounded success in every aspect. Imagine yourself standing on top of Niagara Falls on a perfect day, with your arms open wide, shouting at the Universe, 'Thank you for my life – I love you.'

If you're smiling right now, you've found your destiny. You can see how your life is meant to be, and you like what you see.

Don't waste another second of your precious life. Step into your greatness. Make a decision immediately to pursue that which you now hold in your mind, with desire and faith and unrelenting persistence. Live like you already have it, and celebrate your success.

What you fight for, you get to keep.

Rocky Warren

FIGHTING TIPS

Commit to paper

This is the shortest Fighting Tip in the book, but it is also the most powerful.

Write down on paper exactly what it is you're after, and write it in the present tense.

If you want money, write down, 'My wealth gets greater every day. In 12 months time my bank account will have increased to $1 million.' And date it.

If you're after your perfect weight, write down, 'My weight becomes closer to perfect every day. In six months time my body will be at its perfect weight.' And date it.

If you're a salesperson and you'd like more sales, write down, 'I am a terrific salesperson and my sales increase weekly. In nine months time I'll be recognised financially as the company's top salesperson'. And, of course, date it.

Make sure your goals are achievable and believable to YOU.

When you commit your thoughts and dreams to paper, you're making yourself accountable. And when you put your commitments somewhere you can see and read them every day, you're ensuring that these thoughts are given the focus they require to manifest.

Look at these commitments as often as possible. Ten times a day if you can. And think about how great you'll feel once you have what it is you want. The more often you send these thoughts and good feelings out to the Universe, the quicker the Law of Attraction will work on sending you that which vibrates on the same level. And I'm sure by now you know what that means.

You may not always get exactly what you want. Or it may not be in the time frame you've selected. But if your bank account increased to $800,000 in 15 months, would you be upset? Or if you lost 10 kilos in eight months and only had two or three to go to reach your perfect weight, would you be feeling down? I think not.

Commit to paper and you commit to success.

THE WARM-DOWN

I usually sit on the shower floor and let the water cover my body. I've had the congratulatory kisses and handshakes from well-wishers and I now try to wind down from such an exhilarating experience. The most important words have come from my trainer. They're the ones I really wanted to hear. He said to me, 'Son, I'm proud of you. You did good.' Funny how those simple words can mean so much. I guess it's who you look up to that matters.

I now start to contemplate what I've just done, and how it will affect my life. I feel like I've just won the largest lottery of all time. Nothing could possibly be better than this, and nothing could possibly make me feel any better than I do right now. This is one of those places I'll lock away in my mind, and I'll look back on when I need to 'find that place' later in life.

The fight of your life is now over and you're on top of the world . . . your world. Is it good, or is it good? You now have the techniques and the tools required to have anything and do anything that you want with your life. The best thing, in fact the only thing you should do right now, is apply what you have learned to YOUR life, and start to enjoy the abundance as it presents itself.

It CAN be done. And YOU can do it. It's all about how much you want it. Wallace D. Wattles in his book *The Science of Getting Rich* says, 'Success comes from doing things in a Certain Way.' And of course he's right. My interpretation of that Certain Way is this:

- FOCUS on what you want. Do whatever you have to do to keep what you want at the forefront of your thoughts.

- Go after what you want with DESIRE. Want it so badly that when you see it in your mind, you can taste it, smell it, and almost touch it.
- Have the FAITH that you will have what you want. Never doubt that it's coming, and never doubt that you'll know how to get it.
- Be PERSISTENT. Without persistence all of the above are just words. Have persistent focus. Have persistent desire. And have persistent faith.

When you live your life by the principals of this Certain Way, there is no chance of failure. You will have success upon success upon success. The Laws of the Universe will see to that.

The Law of Non-resistance says, 'Find the easiest path to that which you desire and your enemies will be few.'

I interpret this to mean: if we head in the direction of our dreams and overcome the obstacles with a minimum of fuss, we will not offend anyone along the way. Just like a stream of water running to the ocean, it goes 'around' rocks and trees rather than trying to go 'through' them. It finds the easiest possible path to its destination, and it can't be stopped, no matter what.

Throughout this book you've been exposed to just a few of the Universal Laws that affect and govern your life, whether you're aware of them or not. Do your best to understand these Laws; and I know your life will reward you many times over for your efforts.

We are co-creators of our own lives, and if we don't capitalise on this magical ability with which we've been born, our lives will be created for us by our surroundings, and by the state of the economy, and by the government of the day.

For me, the choice is simple. I will continue to create in my mind that which I desire, and focus on it with faith and persistence, knowing that it can only but manifest into my life.

Unlike my little brother Darrel, and my beloved friend Carol, who never even knew that these Laws existed in their lives, you now have an opportunity to achieve greatness in your life, whatever that may be, without boundaries and without limitation.

Go now and take what is rightly yours from the abundance of everything that there is in our world. Choose whatever it is you want and believe that you can have it. And that you deserve it.

Live your life in that Certain Way and you will never stop attracting to you that which you want. The Law of Attraction is clear: what you focus on with desire, faith and persistence, so you shall have in your life.

This I know for certain.

CAST OF CHARACTERS

The following list is made up of those people whom I've mentioned in my book, who in some way have touched my life. Whether they are an author, a speaker or just a normal, everyday person, I'm listing their information here because I know you can only benefit by reading about them and meeting them as I've had the great fortune to do.

Bob Proctor
Life Success Productions
www.bobproctor.com

Dr Michael Beckwith
Founder of the Agape International Spiritual Centre
www.agapelive.com

Mark Victor Hansen
Co-author of the *Chicken Soup for the Soul* series
www.markvictorhansen.com

Mary Manin Morrissey
New Thought Minister and Spiritual Teacher
www.lifesoulutions.com

Paul Martinelli
President of Life Success Consulting
www.thepowerofmentorship.com

Doug Wead
Author of *The Raising of a President*
www.dougwead.com

Gerry Robert
Author of *The Millionaire Mindset*
www.gerryrobert.com

Wendy Soderman
Teacher and founder of the Ideal School (and mother
of Korey)
www.idealelementary.com

Napoleon Hill
Author of *Think and Grow Rich*
www.naphill.org

1) Conceive it.
2) what does success look like for you?

Acknowledgements

Thank you to those who have profoundly inspired me over the last few years and given me the vision and courage to write this book: Bob Proctor, Dr Michael Beckwith, Mary Morrissey, Paul Martinelli, Mark Victor Hansen, Gerry Robert, Cynthia Kersey, Lisa Jiminez, Steve Siebold, Dawn Andrews, Rhonda Byrne, Wendy Soderman, Selwa Anthony and Sharon King. Oh, and of course Oprah.

You may not know it, but you have all played an integral role in helping to create the person I am today. For this, I will be eternally grateful.

Rocky Warren was born in Sydney, Australia, where he still resides. He has held many titles in his 47 years, including:

* Marketing Genius from 14 years of 'playing' in the advertising industry. His agency was called A Touch of Marketing, or ATOM for short.
* Financial Guru from his last 8 years in the finance industry. He currently owns and runs The Sydney Home Loan Centre.
* NSW Featherweight Champion from his boxing days. He had 48 professional fights. His ring name was 'The Fighting Machine'.

While he accepts all three titles readily, he claims to have really only 'earned' the one from boxing.

Rocky is a recent graduate of the Bill Gove Speech Workshop, one of the most prestigious public speaking courses in the world, and is currently under the mentorship of its president, Steve Siebold.

For more information visit www.rockywarren.net or www.thefighterwithin.com